Thinking Critically: Illegal Immigration

Bonnie Szumski and Jill Karson

San Diego, CA

About the Authors

Bonnie Szumski has been an editor and author of nonfiction books for twenty-five years. Jill Karson has been an editor and author of nonfiction books for young adults for fifteen years.

For more information, contact:
ReferencePoint Press, Inc.
PO Box 27779
San Diego, CA 92198
www.ReferencePointPress.com

Picture Credits:
Cover credit: Thinkstock Images
A. Guillotte: 8, 16, 21, 29, 37, 45, 50, 58, 65

LIBRARY OF CONGRESS CATALOGING-IN-PUBLICATION DATA

Szumski, Bonnie, 1958-
  Thinking critically : illegal immigration / by Bonnie Szumski and Jill Karson.
     pages cm. — (Thinking critically series)
  Includes bibliographical references and index.
  ISBN-13: 978-1-60152-626-7 (hardback)
  ISBN-10: 1-60152-626-1 (hardback)
  1. Illegal aliens—United States—Juvenile literature. I. Karson, Jill. II. Title.
  JV6483.S98 2014
  364.1'370973—dc23
                                                                  2013035556

Contents

Foreword

"Literacy is the most basic currency of the knowledge economy we're living in today." Barack Obama (at the time a senator from Illinois) spoke these words during a 2005 speech before the American Library Association. One question raised by this statement is: What does it mean to be a literate person in the twenty-first century?

E.D. Hirsch Jr., author of *Cultural Literacy: What Every American Needs to Know*, answers the question this way: "To be culturally literate is to possess the basic information needed to thrive in the modern world. The breadth of the information is great, extending over the major domains of human activity from sports to science."

But literacy in the twenty-first century goes beyond the accumulation of knowledge gained through study and experience and expanded over time. Now more than ever literacy requires the ability to sift through and evaluate vast amounts of information and, as the authors of the Common Core State Standards state, to "demonstrate the cogent reasoning and use of evidence that is essential to both private deliberation and responsible citizenship in a democratic republic."

The Thinking Critically series challenges students to become discerning readers, to think independently, and to engage and develop their skills as critical thinkers. Through a narrative-driven, pro/con format, the series introduces students to the complex issues that dominate public discourse—topics such as gun control and violence, social networking, and medical marijuana. All chapters revolve around a single, pointed question such as Can Stronger Gun Control Measures Prevent Mass Shootings?, or Does Social Networking Benefit Society?, or Should Medical Marijuana Be Legalized? This inquiry-based approach introduces student researchers to core issues and concerns on a given topic. Each chapter includes one part that argues the affirmative and one part that argues the negative—all written by a single author. With the single-author format the predominant arguments for and against an issue can be synthesized into clear, accessible discussions supported by details and evidence including relevant facts, direct quotes, current examples, and statistical illustrations. All volumes include focus questions to guide students as they read each pro/con discussion, a list of key facts, and an annotated list of related organizations and websites for conducting further research.

The authors of the Common Core State Standards have set out the particular qualities that a literate person in the twenty-first century must have. These include the ability to think independently, establish a base of knowledge across a wide range of subjects, engage in open-minded but discerning reading and listening, know how to use and evaluate evidence, and appreciate and understand diverse perspectives. The new Thinking Critically series supports these goals by providing a solid introduction to the study of pro/con issues.

Illegal Immigration

In the television show *30 Days,* Morgan Spurlock, a documentary film-maker and the director of the film *Super Size Me,* asks people from two different viewpoints to live with one another for thirty days. The idea is that by meeting and talking firsthand with someone on the other side of a debate, a theoretical issue will gain a human face and give participants on both sides a different perspective. In season two of the series, Spurlock asked a member of the vigilante group Minuteman Civil Defense Corps to live with an illegal immigrant family in East Los Angeles. The Minuteman group voluntarily patrols the US-Mexico border looking for illegal immigrants and tipping off the US Border Patrol when they spot them.

At the start of the episode, the Minuteman, Frank, is adamant that the only right that illegal immigrants to the United States should have is "the right to be deported."[1] Like many in the United States who oppose illegal immigration, Frank holds strong views. His opinion is strong, he avers, because he also was an immigrant—albeit legal—when his family immigrated to the United States after escaping from Cuba in the 1950s. During the time of the Cold War, the United States allowed Cuban citizens to immigrate to escape political repression.

Stepping into Another's Shoes

When Frank enters the world of East Los Angeles to begin living in a 500 square foot (46 sq. m) apartment with the Gonzales family—two parents and five children—he remains convinced that his position on illegal immigration will remain unchanged. Spurlock has told Frank he must adhere to three rules: he must leave behind any personal identification, move in with the Gonzaleses for thirty days, and work as a day laborer. At the first meeting between the two sides, each outlines its position. The Gonzales parents explain why they have come to the United States—to support their family and make a better life for their children. Frank articulates why he thinks the Gonzaleses should go back to Mexico and apply to enter the country legally. For their part, the Gonzales family explains that it would be highly unlikely that the United States would grant them citizenship as the list of Mexicans waiting to enter legally is already years long.

As the episode progresses, Frank (and the television audience) becomes familiar with how the parents, Rigoberto and Paty, must work to take care of their family. Rigoberto works odd jobs, and Paty collects cans and bottles for recycling. Frank begins to understand that the two are not taking government handouts or American jobs, as he believed at the start of the show. He sees that the two rely on their own ingenuity and long hours of labor to get by.

In the final part of the season, Frank goes to visit relatives of the Gonzaleses in Mexico. There, he and the audience see firsthand the desperate poverty of the people in Mexico and gain a deeper understanding of the "push" factor—the economic pressure that drives Mexicans to enter the United States illegally. Frank says that he has gained a deeper understanding of the immigration issue and that he may even no longer participate in the Minuteman group when he gets back home.

At the end of the thirty-day period, it is clear that Frank and the Gonzales family have grown together and become friends, with Frank pledging to sponsor the family when and if they seek citizenship. Though Frank remains a Minuteman, he works on the legislative end of the issue rather than patrolling the border.

A Human Story

As the show so vividly illustrates, the illegal immigration issue is a difficult one. Across the southern US border lies a country of 112 million people, 43 percent of whom are very poor and desperate to improve their

Unauthorized Immigrant Population

As of January 2011, the estimated unauthorized immigrant population in the United States totaled 11,510,000, according to the US Department of Homeland Security's Office of Immigration Statistics. The ten states with the largest unauthorized immigrant populations, and their numbers, are shown here in red. The remaining 3.1 million unauthorized immigrants are scattered in other states.

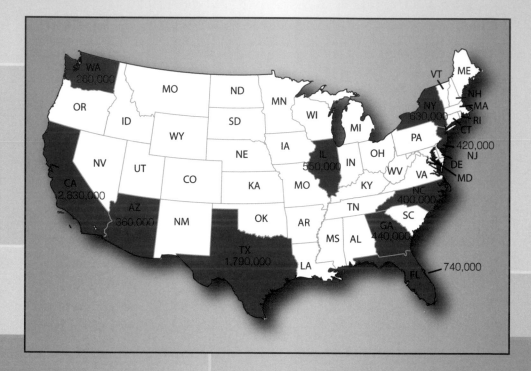

Note: Estimated unauthorized immigrant population in other states totals 3.1 million.

Source: Michael Hoefer et al., US Department of Homeland Security, Office of Immigration Statistics, "Estimates of the Unauthorized Immigrant Population Residing in the United States: January 2011," March 2012. www.dhs.gov.

lives and the lives of their children. The human story that propels illegal immigration is a classic American story: the desire of new immigrants to leave the poverty and repression of their home country and pull themselves out of poverty through the power of sheer hard work and frugal, decent living.

On the other hand, most nations exert some sort of control over their borders; they have rules about who can enter legally and in what numbers. The United States sets limits for how many immigrants can legally enter and from which countries. Because of Latin America's proximity to the United States, millions more enter the country illegally each year, jumping the line of others applying for legal entry.

US immigration laws seem to reinforce the ambiguity the nation feels toward the millions of people who enter the country illegally. Beginning in 1986, the Immigration Reform and Control Act made any immigrant who had illegally entered the country before 1982 eligible for amnesty but made it a crime to hire an illegal immigrant. Then, between 1996 and 2005, the government cracked down on immigration, attempting to limit legal citizenship and increase deportation of those who entered illegally.

More recently, between 2010 and 2013, members of both houses of Congress have proposed and debated variations of a bill known as the DREAM Act. This act would provide a path to citizenship for children brought to the country illegally by their parents. While congressional action on the DREAM Act remained stalled, President Barack Obama instituted the Deferred Action for Childhood Arrivals program in 2012. The deferment allows a five-year path to permanent residency for young people who, with their families, entered the United States illegally as children. Under the law, young adults must have been in the United States since the end of 2011, have entered the country before the age of sixteen, and have either graduated from a US high school or obtained a general equivalency diploma. The law is meant to acknowledge the many children of illegals who have been attending school and working hard to become contributing members of American society. The law also has a grandfather clause: those young people who were deported prior to 2012 for noncriminal reasons would be allowed to reenter the country. Such a change of heart reflects the difficulty of denying citizenship to so many people who, sometimes for many years, have worked and lived illegally in the United States. For many children of illegals, the United States is the only nation they remember living in.

How Big a Problem?

No one knows exactly how many illegals are living in the United States for the simple fact that it is impossible to count people who want to remain hidden. The investment company Bear Stearns Asset Management Inc. believes the number of illegal immigrants in the United States may be as high as 20 million people. The most commonly cited statistics, however, estimate the number to be between 11 million and 12 million. For example, according to a 2013 report from the Pew Research Center an estimated 11.7 million immigrants are living in the United States illegally.

Among the US illegal immigrant population are people from countries around the world. However, the vast majority—almost two-thirds—arrive from Mexico and Central America. Others come from India, South America, and Canada.

Reducing Illegal Immigration?

The states with the largest number of illegals are California and Texas, followed by Florida and Arizona. California, Texas, and Arizona have made massive efforts to increase the safety and impermeability of their borders by asking the federal government to add Border Patrol agents and by spending millions on improving the wall between Mexico and the United States. Some attribute a decrease in illegal immigration to these efforts. Others credit such diverse factors as the US economic recession and falling fertility rates in Mexico. According to a 2010 Pew Research Center report,

> the annual inflow of unauthorized immigrants to the United States was nearly two-thirds smaller in the March 2007 to March 2009 period than it had been from March 2000 to March 2005. This sharp decline has contributed to an overall reduction of 8 percent in the number of unauthorized immigrants currently living in the US—to 11.1 million in March 2009 from a peak of 12 million in March 2007, according to the estimates. The decrease represents the first significant reversal in the growth of this population over the past two decades.[2]

However, a September 2013 Pew Research Center report suggests that the US population of unauthorized immigrants might be on the upswing. "The sharp decline in the U.S. population of unauthorized immigrants that accompanied the 2007–2009 recession has bottomed out, and the number may be rising again,"[3] the Pew Research Hispanic Trends Project states. According to the Pew analysis, the illegal immigrant population reached about 11.7 million in March 2012, which is still below the 2007 peak of 12 million but represents a slight increase over more recent estimates of just over 11 million.

Many involved in the debate argue that illegal immigration is an economic issue that cannot be resolved by building bigger fences or increasing deportations. A simple fact is that many industries in the United States rely on illegal immigrant workers (the majority of whom are from Mexico and Central America), largely because Americans either cannot live on the salary offered or will not take such menial jobs. Illegal immigrants dominate in the areas of food service, agriculture, and landscaping. Citizens benefit from these low-paid, low-skilled workers as well. The 2004 film *A Day Without a Mexican* attempts to imagine what the United States would look like if all illegal Mexicans were to disappear; it reveals just how dependent Americans are on this workforce. Such dependence highlights citizens' own contradictory feelings and actions on the subject of illegal immigration.

Chapter One

How Does Illegal Immigration Affect the Economy?

Illegal Immigration Harms the US Economy

- Illegal immigrants take jobs away from American citizens and drive down wages.
- Illegals are a burden on the American taxpayer because they use social services such as health care, food stamps, and low-cost housing without paying enough back in taxes to offset the cost.
- The children of illegals place an unfair burden on the education system.

The Debate at a Glance

Illegal Immigration Is Essential to the US Economy

- Illegal immigrants mostly take unskilled or low-level jobs that US citizens do not want.
- The money illegal immigrants provide to Social Security helps support the aging US population.
- Because illegals are afraid to access many social services that they pay into through their jobs, they help subsidize these services for others.

Illegal Immigration Harms the US Economy

"The defenders of illegal aliens . . . often assert that illegal aliens only take jobs unwanted by U.S. workers. This is patently false because they are working in jobs in which U.S. workers are also employed—whether in construction, agricultural harvesting or service professions."

—The Federation for American Immigration Reform (FAIR), a private organization that works to reform immigration laws and to prevent illegal immigration.

Federation for American Immigration Reform, "Illegal Aliens Taking U.S. Jobs (2013)," March 2013. www.fairus.org.

Consider these questions as you read:

1. People on both sides of the debate agree that some job loss occurs because of illegal immigration, but they disagree on the severity of the impact. How important are job losses in the debate over illegal immigration's impact on the US economy? Explain.
2. Some commentators believe that Americans would be willing to take menial jobs if they offered higher pay. Do you agree or disagree? Why?
3. Why does the author think that America is ambivalent about illegal immigration? Do you agree or disagree? Explain your answer.

Editor's note: The discussion that follows presents common arguments made in support of this perspective, reinforced by facts, quotes, and examples taken from various sources.

Illegal immigrants hurt the US economy and the American worker in several ways. One of the most devastating is that illegals take jobs away from citizens and legal residents. Because they are often willing to take less money than others would charge—and in some cases far less than minimum wage—illegal immigrants drive down wages so that citizens cannot compete with them.

Because of the difficulty of counting and verifying the illegal population, it is difficult to quantify how many jobs go to illegal immigrants that might otherwise have gone to citizens. Reasonable estimates, such as from the Pew Research Center's Hispanic Trends Project (formerly the Pew Hispanic Center), puts the number of illegals in the US workforce at about 11.5 million. The competition for work only worsens for citizens when illegals are competing for scarce jobs. A 2012 report by the Center for Immigration Studies (CIS) found that, since January 2009, 2 million immigrants—both legal and illegal—have gained employment, but employment of native-born US citizens only rose by 1 million during the same period. Those unemployed citizens must often go on welfare to live at a subsistence level while illegals are benefiting from a job an American citizen should have.

Employers Are Motivated by Greed

Illegal immigrants are preferred over citizens because of the almighty dollar. Employers find that illegals will work for less than their citizen counterparts, an attractive option in construction, hospitality, tourism, and agribusiness—all of which rely heavily on unskilled workers. As the anti–illegal immigration organization FAIR puts it,

> If the hiring of illegal alien workers is prevalent in a sector of the economy, as it has become the case in seasonal crop agriculture, the willingness of foreign workers to accept lower wages because of their illegal status acts to depress wages and working conditions for all workers in that occupation. This in turn makes employment in that sector less attractive to U.S. workers who have other options.[4]

The main problem, then, is not the false idea that American citizens are unwilling to work in menial jobs but that these jobs are not offered at even minimum wage. If immigration laws were more consistently enforced so that employers could not get away with hiring illegals, wages would go up. Once wages improved, more Americans would take the work. In 2006, for example, federal agents raided Swift & Company meatpacking plants in six states looking for illegals. Illegal employees had stolen the identities of lawful US citizens, using their Social Security numbers to obtain jobs at the plants. About thirteen hundred workers were arrested and taken to detention facilities, where most were deported. After the raids, Swift management raised wages by $1.95 an hour, and once it did, the plants attracted plenty of US workers. Enforcement of immigration laws is the key to thwarting American companies that hire illegals and to ending the underground economy in which illegals flourish. Without jobs, there would be no illegal immigration.

Other false beliefs proliferate in the argument over illegal immigration and the economy. Another persistent assertion is that companies that are forced to pay higher wages would pass these costs on to the consumer, effectively harming the American worker and the economy. This argument ignores the fact that higher costs would easily be offset by more Americans working at decent jobs. An article by Philip Martin of the University of California, Davis examines the impact of such logic on the agricultural industry. Martin found that the price of fresh produce would go up about $9 a year—a pittance—if illegals were paid minimum wage. Consumer impact would be negligible because the cost of labor is still one of the least expensive factors in bringing goods to market.

> "If the hiring of illegal alien workers is prevalent in a sector of the economy, as it has become the case in seasonal crop agriculture, the willingness of foreign workers to accept lower wages because of their illegal status acts to depress wages and working conditions for all workers in that occupation."[4]
>
> —FAIR, a private organization that works to reform immigration laws and to prevent illegal immigration.

Illegals Are a Drain on the Economy

The underground illegal economy hurts US workers in other, less obvious ways. While they are here, illegals access the many free or low-cost public

Government Spends Millions on Services for Undocumented Immigrants

Illegal immigration places a great burden on the American taxpayers. Average government expenditures for benefits and services provided to undocumented immigrant families totals $24,721 per household per year.

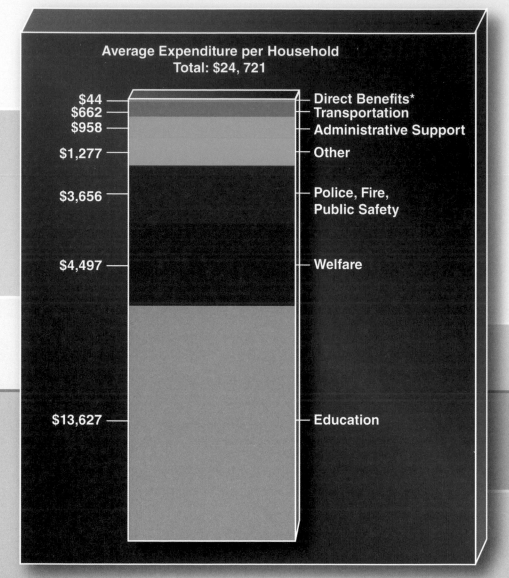

Average Expenditure per Household
Total: $24, 721

- $44 — Direct Benefits*
- $662 — Transportation
- $958 — Administrative Support
- $1,277 — Other
- $3,656 — Police, Fire, Public Safety
- $4,497 — Welfare
- $13,627 — Education

* Direct benefits include Social Security, Medicare, unemployment insurance, and worker's compensation.

Source: Robert Rector and Jason Richwine, "The Fiscal Cost of Unlawful Immigrants and Amnesty to the U.S. Taxpayer," The Heritage Foundation, May 6, 2013. www.heritage.org; U.S. Census Bureau, 2010 Current Population Survey, and U.S. Bureau of Labor Statistics, 2010 Consumer Expenditure Survey.

services intended for citizens and paid for by the American tax dollar. Many argue that because illegals earn so little money and are afraid to access social services that they end up putting more into the economy than what they take out of it. This is simply inaccurate. Illegals do not pay their fair share in taxes to offset the public services they use. They are dependent on federal aid programs because they receive low wages and usually no benefits. They must rely on free public clinics, for example, funded by the American taxpayer. According to FAIR, the cost of illegal immigration is roughly $113 billion a year, nearly $29 billion at the federal level and $84 billion at the state and local level. FAIR's 2011 report found that the taxes collected from illegal immigrant workers is far below these expenditures—they contribute close to $13 billion, resulting in a net loss to taxpayers of about $100 billion a year.

In cities where illegal immigration is rampant, the burden on taxpayers is almost criminal. Los Angeles County supervisor Michael Antonovich found that the total cost for illegal immigrants to county taxpayers was more than $1.6 billion in 2010, including health care and public safety costs. That did not even include the hundreds of millions spent on educating the children of illegals. The fact that many of these children are US citizens begs the question—the only reason those children are citizens is because their parents sneaked over the border to intentionally give birth to them in the United States. A spokesperson for Antonovich, Tony Bell, said, "The problem is illegal immigration. . . . Their parents evidently immigrated here in order to get on social services. . . . We can no longer afford to be the HMO capital of the world."[5]

Texas is another state in which illegals are harming the economy. According to a study released in 2011 by the CIS, 70 percent of illegal immigrants in Texas receive welfare benefits—mostly food assistance and Medicaid—that are directly derived from the benefits granted to their US-born children.

The US government is so ambivalent about illegal immigration that it is virtually impossible to gain any control over the problem. In the 1982 decision *Plyler v. Doe*, the Supreme Court ruled that it is unconstitutional to deny the children of illegal immigrants an education at a public school. This decision translated into a big invitation to "come on over the border

17

and we'll take care of your kids" at the expense of US citizens. According to a study by FAIR, nearly half of the estimated $113 billion-a-year cost of illegal immigration is for education. This places a great financial burden on states, such as California, with large populations of illegals. The total annual cost in California to educate children of illegals is estimated at $21.8 billion.

The US Dollar Bolsters the Mexican Economy

Although it is easy to see that illegals benefit from services meant for US citizens, they are also not contributing to the US economy in other ways. Instead of recirculating the money they earn back into the US economy, they often send any excess monies back to their country of origin, usually Mexico. Some estimate that $50 billion a year flows out of the United States. Illegals are simply adding insult to injury with these actions: not only do they not bother to wait to become citizens, but they are truly loyal to their country of origin, showing no respect for the United States. By not enforcing immigration laws, the United States is actually supporting the Mexican economy to the detriment of its own.

The Colorado Alliance for Immigration Reform sums up the many ways that illegal immigration harms the US economy:

> The economic and social consequences of illegal immigration . . . are staggering. . . . Illegal aliens have cost billions of taxpayer-funded dollars for medical services. . . . Immigration is a net drain on the economy; corporate interests reap the benefits of cheap labor, while taxpayers pay the infrastructural cost. . . . $60 billion dollars are earned by illegal aliens in the U.S. each year. One of Mexico's largest revenue streams (after exports and oil sales) consists of money sent home by legal immigrants and illegal aliens working in the U.S. . . . This is a massive transfer of wealth from America—essentially from America's displaced working poor—to Mexico.[6]

The United States can no longer afford unchecked illegal immigration.

Illegal Immigration Is Essential to the US Economy

"The research has found that immigrants—including the poor, uneducated ones coming from south of the border—have a big positive impact on the economy over the long run, bolstering the profitability of American firms [and] reducing the prices of some products and services."

—Eduardo Porter, reporter for the *New York Times*.

Eduardo Porter, "Immigration and American Jobs," *New York Times*, October 19, 2012. www.nytimes.com.

Consider these questions as you read:

1. Some argue that illegal immigration keeps prices on consumer goods low. Do you think Americans would be willing to pay more for groceries, for example, to eliminate illegal immigration? Why or why not?
2. Whereas this essay argues that illegals send very little money back to Latin America because they spend most of their wages on essentials, the previous essay argued that illegals send most of their money back to Latin America. Who do you think is right? Explain your answer.
3. Should illegal immigrants be eligible to receive the benefits that they cannot now receive but pay for in taxes, such as Social Security and Medicare? Why or why not?

Editor's note: The discussion that follows presents common arguments made in support of this perspective, reinforced by facts, quotes, and examples taken from various sources.

Poll after poll show that the American public believes illegal immigration is bad. In a 2010 *New York Times*/CBS News poll, for example, 74 percent of respondents said illegal immigrants weakened the economy, and only 17 percent believed they had a positive impact. Yet economists are unanimous in contending that both legal and illegal immigration provide a net gain for the economy. Despite what the average citizen thinks, then, the American economy runs, in part, on the backs of illegal immigrants. Illegal immigrants are hardworking and provide a source of cheap labor that is essential, especially in industries that rely on unskilled labor, such as farming, construction, and meatpacking. The benefits provided by these underground workers greatly outweigh the liabilities.

Consumers and Employers Benefit

American citizens benefit from illegal immigrants and the low-cost labor they provide through lower costs of consumer goods. Businesses pass on the labor savings to consumers in the form of lower supermarket prices, for example. A reduction in seasonal agricultural workers would cause consumer costs to skyrocket. In San Diego County, where an estimated two hundred thousand illegal immigrants are employed, farms depend heavily on immigrant labor. Erik Larson of the San Diego Farm Bureau says that without immigrant labor, most farms in the county would disappear. "The avocado trees that blanket the hills of Fallbrook and Valley Center, those all go away without farm workers. So do the oranges here in San Pasqual Valley, the nurseries of San Marcos and Vista, the Carlsbad flower fields,"[7] says Larson. This would also be true for the construction industry, which relies on undocumented workers for unskilled labor. American citizens would find themselves paying much more for new housing without illegal immigrants. By keeping the cost of

> "Undocumented immigrants contribute to the U.S. economy through their investments and consumption of goods and services; filling of millions of essential worker positions resulting in subsidiary job creation, increased productivity and lower costs of goods and services; and unrequited contributions to Social Security, Medicare and unemployment insurance programs."[9]
>
> —Francine J. Lipman, a professor of law and economics at Chapman University.

US Industries Depend on Immigrant Labor

Construction, agriculture, leisure and hospitality, and manufacturing have many low-skill, low-pay jobs, and many of these are filled by undocumented immigrants. Representatives of some of these industries say they could not function without these workers. The chart shows which industries depend most on such immigrant labor.

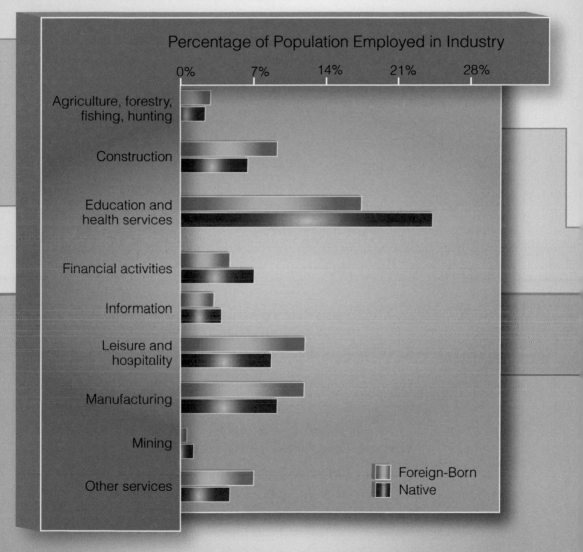

Percentage of Population Employed in Industry

Foreign-Born
Native

Source: Danielle Kurtzleben, "What Immigrants Mean to the US Economy, in 5 Charts," *U.S. News & World Report*, February 4, 2013, www.usnews.com.

goods down, illegal laborers help American companies compete. This is why American employers continue to hire illegals, even though they are risking fines and the scrutiny of federal immigration officials.

With easy access to cheap labor, more businesses are created, meaning more competition that drives down overall prices. Reporter Eduardo Porter notes in an article for the *New York Times* that in countries with little or no source of cheap labor, fewer businesses flourish. Norway has far fewer restaurants than does the United States, for example, largely because it has no source of cheap labor. In addition, cheap labor benefits native workers. While many businesses, such as construction companies, hire illegals to do the unskilled labor, supervisors and skilled workers are nearly always native workers. The same is true in restaurants: the kitchen is often filled with illegal dishwashers and assistant cooks, but the more highly skilled jobs and all wait staff are filled by native workers whose facility in English is required to communicate. So, not only do more businesses flourish because of the availability of cheap labor, but opportunities for native workers also increase. Giovanni Peri, an economist at the University of California, Davis, has estimated that immigrants who entered the United States between 1990 and 2007 increased the national income per worker by about $5,400 a year on average, in 2007 dollars. Porter concludes that illegal immigrants increase new business by "providing employers with a new labor source and creating more opportunities for investment and jobs."[8]

If the enforcement of immigration laws succeeded in decreasing the number of undocumented workers, then the number of new businesses that depend on cheap labor would also decrease. The loss of these businesses would mean an overall loss in the tax base.

Illegals Contribute to the Tax Base

Illegals are an economic force that put money back into the US economy through sales taxes and property taxes that they pay without receiving any of the benefits, such as government services and Social Security, which citizens receive when they contribute. Though they send some of their money back to their country of origin, it is typically only about 15 percent of their income. Most of their wages are spent on rent, food, and other essentials. Raul Hinojosa, a professor at the University of California, Los Angeles, estimates that 90 percent of the wages of undocumented workers are spent in United States.

In fact, the argument that the United States subsidizes Latin America's economy is misguided. Some economists actually estimate that Latin America subsidizes the United States. Latin Americans, for example, hold 1.9 trillion assets in the United States and invest more than $100 billion each year in the US market. This is far more money than flows back across the border from illegal immigrants and dwarfs the amount of money that the United States gives in aid to these countries. Americans need to understand that they actually benefit far more from illegal immigration than do the countries of Latin America.

> "As the baby boomers retire, the post-boom generation's burden to finance their retirement is greatly alleviated by undocumented immigrants."[10]
>
> —Adam Davidson, the cofounder of NPR's series *Planet Money.*

Even the children of illegals who are born in the United States are an economic boon to the nation. Every one of these children will grow into tax-paying members of society and add their brains and brawn to the economy. This will become especially important as America's low birthrate makes it difficult to maintain social services, especially for the increasingly elderly population.

In addition to providing a workforce for the aging population, illegal immigrants contribute to the tax base. US tax laws grant Individual Taxpayer Identification Numbers to aliens who do not qualify to work in the United States and do not qualify for Social Security. The Internal Revenue Service (IRS) has three basic requirements for people receiving these numbers: 1) they have to be an alien, 2) they do not qualify to work in the United States or have a Social Security number, and 3) they owe taxes in the United States. The IRS keeps tax information confidential and, with a few exceptions, does not share that information with other government agencies. Illegal aliens contribute to programs such as Medicare, Social Security, veterans benefits, and more, even though they often cannot ever use them. They are, however, subject to the same payroll deductions as citizens. According to Social Security Administration estimates, in 2010 illegal immigrants paid about $12 billion into the system (with fraudulent Social Security numbers or after overstaying work visas). Those illegals who contribute to Social Security are not eligible to receive the benefits unless they gain legal status.

Moreover, according to the Center for American Progress, if 70 percent of illegal immigrants become legal, they would contribute $500 billion net over the next thirty-six years, which would ease the fiscal burden of baby boomers drawing Social Security benefits. According to Francine J. Lipman, a professor of law and economics at Chapman University,

> Undocumented immigrants contribute to the U.S. economy through their investments and consumption of goods and services; filling of millions of essential worker positions resulting in subsidiary job creation, increased productivity and lower costs of goods and services; and unrequited contributions to Social Security, Medicare and unemployment insurance programs.[9]

A Myriad of Financial Contributions

Thus, the financial contributions illegals make far outweigh what they take in the form of food assistance and other benefits. Adam Davidson, the cofounder of National Public Radio's series *Planet Money,* explains how illegal immigrants greatly subsidize American retirees:

> As the baby boomers retire, the post-boom generation's burden to finance their retirement is greatly alleviated by undocumented immigrants. Stephen Goss, chief actuary for the Social Security Administration, told me that undocumented workers contribute about $15 billion a year to Social Security through payroll taxes. They only take out $1 billion (very few undocumented workers are eligible to receive benefits). Over the years, undocumented workers have contributed up to $300 billion, or nearly 10 percent, of the $2.7 trillion Social Security Trust Fund.[10]

Although it is true that illegal immigration may hamper some entry-level, unskilled citizens from obtaining jobs, this impact is small compared with the many financial benefits illegals provide. It is time for Americans to understand the truth about illegal immigration and embrace it as part of what makes the economy strong.

Chapter Two

How Does Illegal Immigration Impact America's Safety and Security?

Illegal Immigration Threatens the Safety and Security of Americans

- As of 2010, fifty-five thousand criminal illegals were imprisoned, making illegal immigrant crime a major US issue.
- Mexican drug-trafficking organizations use criminal aliens to import drugs into the United States.
- The US-Mexico border has become a dangerous place because of illegal immigration.
- The number of illegals entering the United States from hostile nations has increased, raising the likelihood of a terrorist attack.

The Debate at a Glance

Illegal Immigration Does Not Threaten the Safety and Security of Americans

- Border towns, such as San Diego, California, and El Paso, Texas, are some of the safest cities in the United States.
- Though illegal immigration in Arizona is at historic highs, the violent crime rate is down by 20 percent.
- Studies have shown that the more immigrants, both legal and illegal, that a city has, the safer that city is.
- Criminal justice monies are wasted on arresting illegal immigrants rather than being used to have police officers find and prosecute violent crime.

Illegal Immigration Threatens the Safety and Security of Americans

"Many illegal immigrants come here precisely because they are criminals and they find America a target-rich environment."

—Writer Roger D. McGrath, writer and historian.

Roger D. McGrath, "Double Down: Illegal Aliens and Crime," *Chronicles*, July 12, 2010. www.chronicles magazine.org.

Consider these questions as you read:

1. If criminal aliens are imprisoned and then released to commit more crimes, how might this statistic inflate the overall criminal alien crime statistics?
2. The essay blames an increase in teenage drug use on illegal immigration? Do you agree or disagree? Why?
3. The recent Boston Marathon bombing is cited as a reason to curb illegal immigration. Do you think this argument is sound? Why or why not?

Editor's note: The discussion that follows presents common arguments made in support of this perspective, reinforced by facts, quotes, and examples taken from various sources.

Unchecked illegal immigration increases crime in the United States. In the online magazine *Chronicles,* writer and historian Roger D. McGrath talks about how his area of Ventura County, California, is rife with crimes committed by illegal aliens. In fact, many criminals in California jails who have been arrested for crimes such as murder, kidnapping, and rape are also illegal aliens. The problem is only growing worse.

Disturbing Statistics

A 2011 report by the US Government Accountability Office analyzed the scope of criminal activity by illegal immigrants. The number of criminal aliens in federal prisons in 2010 was roughly 55,000, which represents a 7 percent increase since 2005. In 2009, 296,000 criminal aliens were incarcerated in state and local prisons. These numbers may seem surprising until one understands that the average criminal alien is arrested seven times. Once aliens are arrested and deported, they often return and commit new crimes.

The number and variety of serious crimes committed by illegals is astonishing: 65 percent for immigration offenses, 50 percent for drug arrests, 35 percent for assault, 19 percent for weapons violations, and 8 percent for homicides. In a nutshell, illegal immigrants are free to commit crimes in the United States, and once jailed, they become the responsibility of the United States to warehouse and feed while they are in prison. The United States must take immediate action to stop this trend.

According to a Congressional Research Service report issued in August 2012, between October 2008 and July 2011 close to 160,000 illegal aliens were arrested by local authorities and identified as deportable. Yet a lack of political will to send these immigrants back home meant many were released back onto the streets. Close to one-sixth of these illegals were again arrested for a variety of crimes. Just a sampling from the first half of 2013 included abduction, drug offenses, the rape of an eleven-year-old child, and murder.

Some people have argued that this criminal element comprises only a small percentage of the overall illegal population; however, this is not so. California, for example, is home to an estimated 2.4 million illegal aliens, representing 7.1 percent of the state's total population. Yet illegal aliens make up 12.7 percent of the state's incarcerated population. This demonstrates that the number of illegals in prison for committing various crimes is disproportionately large.

Drug Traffickers

Criminal aliens are also responsible for much of the drug traffic into the United States. According to the 2010 *National Drug Threat Assessment* report for the US Department of Justice (DOJ), one in five youths in the United States aged twelve to seventeen has used drugs in the past year. The main drug supplier to these kids are Mexican drug-trafficking organizations (DTOs), with criminal aliens acting as dealers. The DOJ report states that "Mexican DTOs continue to represent the single greatest drug trafficking threat to the United States." The report also called the Mexican DTOs "the predominant wholesale suppliers of illicit drugs in the United States."[11] Our permeable border puts our children and teens at risk by allowing illegals to peddle their wares in the United States.

> "Mexican criminals have penetrated deep into the United States. These Mexican gangsters seem to come and go across our border with impunity and live openly among other illegal aliens—those who come here 'only to work'—in our towns and cities."[12]
>
> —Roger D. McGrath, writer and historian.

Just one example of how illegal alien drug traffickers feel free to operate in the United States is the case of Antonio Medina Arreguin. For several years Arreguin smuggled about 440 pounds (200 kg) of heroin each month into California, with a distribution center in Oxnard. McGrath, who lives near Arreguin's base of operations, says, "We haven't penetrated deep into Mexico; Mexican criminals have penetrated deep into the United States. These Mexican gangsters seem to come and go across our border with impunity and live openly among other illegal aliens—those who come here 'only to work'—in our towns and cities."[12]

In addition to flooding our towns and cities with drugs, Mexican DTOs also bring crime and violence. The DOJ report states that

> although much of the violence attributed to conflicts over control of the smuggling routes has been confined to Mexico, some has occurred in the United States. . . . Violence in the United States . . . has been limited primarily to attacks against alien smuggling organization members and their families—some of whom have sought refuge from violence in Mexico by moving to U.S. border communities such as Phoenix. For example, in recent years, kidnappings in Phoenix have numbered in the hundreds, with 260 in 2007, 299 in 2008, and 267 in 2009.[13]

Many undocumented immigrants who are apprehended in the United States are from countries that are home to known terrorist organizations. The US government, for example, has officially designated Cuba, Iran, Sudan, and Syria as state sponsors of terror. While the numbers fluctuate, undocumented immigrants from these countries are arrested each year.

Number of Aliens Apprehended

Country of Nationality	2002	2003	2004	2005	2006	2007	2008	2009	2010	2011
Afghanistan	85	61	57	55	53	28	74	74	88	106
Algeria	68	202	49	39	50	49	59	53	59	36
Cuba	2,750	2,425	1,831	4,285	5,088	4,931	6,677	4,701	3,947	4,691
Iran	161	425	138	166	215	128	239	277	285	276
Iraq	110	237	135	164	170	138	222	282	267	265
Lebanon	190	953	157	125	260	195	236	216	214	169
Libya	13	19	7	5	10	8	21	13	14	24
Pakistan	1,444	4,083	641	792	721	654	655	575	592	525
Saudi Arabia	122	131	72	40	130	67	87	70	144	123
Sudan	89	90	50	81	74	38	164	196	227	198
Syria	122	369	106	113	151	101	101	87	95	108
Yemen	121	396	88	67	64	106	90	82	129	83

Source: Department of Homeland Security, *2011 Yearbook of Immigration Statistics*, Office of Immigration Statistics, September 2012. www.dhs.gov.

The Terrorism Threat

Drugs and crime pale by comparison with the threat of terrorism posed by illegal immigrants from parts of the world hostile to the United States. Members of al Qaeda and other terrorist groups can enter the country illegally and perpetrate violence against US citizens. In July 2013 the United Nations Office on Drugs and Crime released a report titled *Transnational Organized Crime in Central America and the Caribbean.* This report posits that the US-Mexico border is an open door not only for immigrants but also for "irregular migrants," which could include terrorists associated with al Qaeda, Islamic extremists, and other groups hostile to the United States. The report stated that these "irregulars" from countries such as Somalia, Ethiopia, India, and China travel to Central America, where they cross the US border the same way other illegal immigrants do.

These immigrants pose a different threat, according to Senator John Cornyn from Texas, in a speech during a conference on the border issue:

> "In [2010]—where 445,000 individuals were detained at the southwest border—59,000 came from countries other than Mexico. . . . These included 663 individuals from special-interest countries [because of their suspected ties to terrorism]."[14]
>
> —Senator John Cornyn from Texas.

It's not just that we're seeing immigration across our southern border from countries like Mexico—people seeking to work and provide for their families. . . . Indeed in [2010]—where 445,000 individuals were detained at the southwest border—59,000 came from countries other than Mexico. . . . These included 663 individuals from special-interest countries [because of their suspected ties to terrorism] like Afghanistan, Libya, Pakistan, Somalia, and Yemen and four countries that have been designated by the U.S. Department of State as state-sponsors of terror—Cuba, Iran, Syria, and Sudan.[14]

These illegals are coming from countries that despise the United States, bringing traditions of Islamic fundamentalism and other tenets that support harming the people of this country. Such ideas are not far-fetched, given the recent Boston Marathon bombing. Though the Tsarnaev family legally immigrated to the United States from Chechnya, the mother, a Muslim, preached radical Islamist ideas that her sons embraced. This radical immigrant element exists in the United States and can be recruited for attacks. The two young men responsible for the act of terrorism, Dzhokhar, aged twenty, and his brother, Tamerlan, twenty-six, set off two bombs near the finish line of the Boston Marathon on April 15, 2013, killing 3 people and injuring more than 260 others. Tamerlan was shot and killed by police later that week, and Dzhokhar was arrested following a manhunt that shut down Greater Boston. The FBI believes that the brothers may have been in contact with illegal immigrant radicals who helped coach them on making the bombs and carrying out their plan.

In 2012 the US House Committee on Homeland Security's Subcommittee on Oversight, Investigations, and Management published a report that seconded such views:

> The Congressional Research Service reports that between September 2001 and September 2012 there have been 59 homegrown violent jihadist plots within the United States. Of growing concern and potentially a more violent threat to American citizens is the enhanced ability of Middle East terrorist organizations, aided by their relationships and growing presence in the western Hemisphere, to exploit the Southwest border to enter the United States undetected.[15]

Just one example is the extremely vicious Central American gang Mara Salvatrucha, or MS-13, as it is known. The gang smuggles aliens into the United States, holds illegals for ransom, and has been accused of conspiring with known terrorists, including members of al Qaeda, about how to infiltrate the border. Adnan G. El Shukrijumah, a key al Qaeda leader currently on the FBI's most-wanted list, is known to have met with the MS-13 gang leaders who control smuggling routes into the United States.

Attacks Against Other Illegals

Criminal aliens do not just target US citizens; they also prey on their fellow illegals. According to analysis by the Washington Office on Latin

America, there were 463 illegal immigrant deaths in fiscal year 2012—which translates to about five immigrants dying every four days. Illegals trying to cross the border are often victims of criminal acts that include kidnapping, robbery, sexual violence, and human trafficking. Clearly, stopping criminal aliens should be a high priority. The United States has to stop naively believing in the idea that illegals just want to improve their lives, work hard, and take menial jobs. They want to continue their criminal lifestyle in the United States, where new victims abound.

Illegal Immigration Does Not Threaten the Safety and Security of Americans

"In the past decade, as illegal immigrants were drawn in record numbers by the housing boom, the rate of violent crimes in Phoenix and the entire state fell by more than 20 percent, a steeper drop than in the overall U.S. crime rate."

—Daniel Griswold, *Washington Times* reporter.

Daniel Griswold, "Unfounded Fear of Immigrant Crime Grips Arizona," *Washington Times,* May 25, 2010. www.cato.org.

Consider these questions as you read:

1. This essay disagrees with the previous one, arguing that illegals are here to better their lives, not commit crimes. Comparing and contrasting the arguments, which is more convincing? Defend your answer.
2. This essay offers statistics to prove that Arizona's fear of criminal aliens is based on perception, not reality. Do you think these statistics prove the argument? Why or why not?
3. The two essays in this chapter have very different views about the terrorist threat posed by illegal immigrants. Which argument is more convincing? Why?

Editor's note: The discussion that follows presents common arguments made in support of this perspective, reinforced by facts, quotes, and examples taken from various sources.

If one listens to the propaganda spouted by anti-immigration pundits, the border city of El Paso, Texas, should be one of the most crime-ridden, unsafe cities in the United States. In 2007 the city's poverty rate was 27 percent—twice that of the national average. The city is three-quarters Hispanic—25 percent of its population is foreign-born, and a significant portion of its foreign-born residents are in the United States illegally. What's more, El Paso lies across the border from Ciudad Juárez, one of the most violent and drug-ridden cities in Mexico. In spite of all of these factors, however, El Paso is one of the safest cities in the United States. Surprising? Not to criminologists, who argue that this is typical for a border town. According to Northeastern University criminologist Jack Levin, El Paso is safe because of its immigrants: "If you want to find a safe city, first determine the size of the immigrant population. If the immigrant community represents a large proportion of the population, you're likely in one of the country's safest cities."[16]

> "If you want to find a safe city, first determine the size of the immigrant population. If the immigrant community represents a large proportion of the population, you're likely in one of the country's safest cities."[16]
>
> —Northeastern University criminologist Jack Levin.

Crime Rates Are Low in Border Towns

The vast majority of illegal immigrants in the United States are here for one reason only: to improve their lives and the lives of their children. Anti–illegal immigrant zealots claim that illegals are responsible for committing many, if not all, of the crimes in many areas of the country. Yet the facts contradict this assertion. As numerous studies demonstrate, in border towns (which have the highest numbers of illegal residents) crime rates are low or have dropped.

A study by the Immigration Policy Center (IPC) found that immigrants of all kinds, whether illegal or legal, are more law abiding, commit fewer crimes, and are less likely to be jailed than their citizen counterparts. Ruben G. Rumbaut, the coauthor of the study and a sociology professor at the University of California, Irvine, explains: "The misperception that immigrants, especially illegal immigrants, are responsible for higher crime rates is deeply rooted in American public opinion and is sustained by media anecdotes and popular myth. . . . This perception is not supported empirically. In fact, it is refuted by the preponderance of evidence."[17]

An analyst with the Americas Policy Program of the Center for International Studies makes three major points in support of the view that illegal immigrants are not to blame for US crime rates. He contends that although illegal immigration has reached new highs, crime rates have declined, especially in border towns such as San Diego and El Paso. Likewise, the incarceration rate for foreign-born men between the ages of eighteen and thirty-nine is five times less than that of native-born men in the same age group. Lastly, even though foreign-born men are the least educated and acculturated, they still commit fewer crimes than their native counterparts.

The Myth Adds to the Perception

These facts sometimes have little impact on people's perceptions, especially in places such as Arizona, where the immigration issue is so contentious. The main component of Arizona's immigration law, known as SB 1070, requires police to determine the immigration status of anyone they stop or arrest if they have reason to suspect that the individual might be in the country illegally. Although many decry the law as racist and unconstitutional, in 2012 the US Supreme Court upheld the law's "show me your papers" provision.

Supporters of the law have argued that such measures are needed because the state is rife with property crime and violent crime, much of it committed by illegals. Opponents, on the other hand, have argued that those who draw a connection between illegal immigration and high crime rates do so based on faulty information. Daniel Griswold, director of the Center for Trade Policy Studies at the Cato Institute, says:

> One big problem in the Arizona debate is that the perceptions about immigrants and crime do not square with the most basic data. After years of witnessing a rise in the number of illegal

immigrants in their state, the people of Arizona are in reality less likely to be victims of crime than at any time in the past four decades. . . . The large majority of immigrants who enter the United States, legally and illegally, come here to work and save and support their families. Once inside the country, they want to stay out of trouble and not jeopardize their opportunity to earn income in our relatively free and open economy.[18]

Perception, then, not crime, stirs up emotions in Arizona. According to the most recent statistics from the DOJ, violent crime in Arizona is at the lowest it has been since 1971. In 2010 property crimes fell to their lowest numbers since 1966, while illegal immigration has increased to historic highs. Violent crime throughout the state fell by more than 20 percent—a bigger decrease than the overall US violent crime rate. The same can be said for violence related to drug crimes. Nogales assistant police chief Roy Bermudez argues that "we have not, thank God, witnessed any spillover violence from Mexico. . . . You can look at the crime stats. I think Nogales, Arizona, is one of the safest places to live in all of America."[19]

Could Prosecution Lead to More Crime?

Some argue that Arizona's strict enforcement of immigration law and deportation of illegals may actually lead to an increase in crime. Reporter Spencer S. Hsu wrote in the *Washington Post* that "Arizona's new crackdown on illegal immigration will increase crime in U.S. cities, not reduce it, by driving a wedge between police and immigrant communities. . . . Arizona's law will intimidate crime victims and witnesses who are illegal immigrants and divert police from investigating more serious crimes."[20]

Strict laws such as Arizona's place a burden on law officers to aggressively pursue illegals, at the expense of finding and prosecuting real criminals. According to writer Jason Arvak,

Supporters of the [Arizona] law point out that illegal immigration is a crime. Ok, fair enough. But how serious of a crime is it?

36

Low Crime Rates in El Paso, Texas

The city of El Paso, Texas, is home to a large population of illegal immigrants. Nevertheless, El Paso has lower crime rates than many US cities. When compared to the total of other cities in Texas, El Paso has lower rates of crime in seven out of nine categories including murder, rape, and robbery. This belies the notion that large populations of illegal immigrants are associated with high crime rates.

Crime Rates, 2010	El Paso, Texas	State of Texas
Violent Crime	452.1	450.3
Murder and nonnegligent manslaughter	0.9	5.0
Forcible rape	29.4	30.3
Robbery	70.1	130.6
Aggrivated assult	351.7	284.4
Property crime	2,747.4	3,783.0
Burgurlary	357.1	909.1
Larceny/theft	2,152.2	2,603.3
Motor vehicle theft	238.1	270.5

Rates per 100,000 people

Source: US Department of Justice/Federal Bureau of Investigations, "Crime in the United States," 2011, www.fbi.gov.

Does anyone die or get injured from a poor guy crossing a border looking for work picking tomatoes? Of course not. Yes, some illegal immigrants are criminals or drug runners or human traffickers, but so are a lot of citizens and legal residents. There is no credible evidence I am aware of to support the anti-immigration activists' claim that illegal immigration is uniquely linked to any violent crime. Yet, the effect of the Arizona law is to require police to set aside their work on murders, rapes, and robberies whenever they believe they may have just run into an illegal immigrant and focus instead on confirming or disproving that suspicion.[21]

The Terrorist Threat

The focus on illegal immigrants and crime has led some commentators to go a step further, claiming that those who enter the United States illegally pose a terrorist threat. Yet this does not square with the facts. Most of the illegal population in the United States comes from Mexico, which has no history of terrorism. And although Latinos make up nearly 13 percent of the US prison population, 48 percent of Latino offenders were convicted of immigration crimes, while low-level drug offenses were the second most prevalent charge. What's more, in the past serious terrorism incidents in the United States were not committed by people who crossed the border illegally. According to the American Immigration Council (formerly the American Immigration Law Foundation),

> "Illegal immigrants are not terrorists. They want to come legally to do the jobs Americans don't want, but our broken immigration system doesn't allow that to happen."[22]
>
> —American Immigration Council (formerly the American Immigration Law Foundation), which promotes humane immigration policies.

Illegal immigrants are not terrorists. They want to come legally to do the jobs Americans don't want, but our broken immigration system doesn't allow that to happen. If there were legal channels for these migrants to use, the government could concentrate on identifying the real terrorists. Instead, the government is wasting money and manpower trying to keep out the immigrant workers the U.S. economy needs. That makes the job of finding a terrorist like finding a needle in a haystack.[22]

A terrorist wanting to commit crimes against Americans is going to be much more sophisticated and secretive—and, therefore, elusive—to border agents than the average illegal entering the United States. Although terrorists may want to enter the United States, they will only be caught the way they are caught now, through sophisticated surveillance and tracking measures, not by a border guard in Nogales or Phoenix. The United States has legitimate reasons to reinforce its border, such as making sure that it controls who enters the country and from where. What is clear, however, is that immigration policy should not be guided by the fear of trumped up accusations of an increased crime rate.

Chapter Three

Should Illegal Immigrants Be Offered a Path to Citizenship?

Illegal Immigrants Should Be Offered a Path to Citizenship

- Illegal immigrants have proven through hard work that they deserve a path to citizenship.
- The vast majority of Americans believe illegals should be granted some form of amnesty.
- Amnesty makes good economic sense for the United States.
- Changing demographics will mean that the United States will require a large pool of new workers to take care of the aging baby boomer population.

The Debate at a Glance

Illegal Immigrants Should Not Be Offered a Path to Citizenship

- Past amnesty programs have proven that they fail.
- Amnesty rewards illegal behavior.
- Illegal immigrants granted amnesty are less likely to assimilate.
- Border Patrol measures to control illegal immigration are working.

Illegal Immigrants Should Be Offered a Path to Citizenship

"The National Immigration Law Center calls for passage of broad and humane immigration reform legislation that provides a clear roadmap to first-class citizenship for the 11 million aspiring Americans, including DREAMers, and makes it possible for them to fully integrate into the nation's social and economic fabric, with all the rights and responsibilities entailed in full integration."

—NILC engages in policy analysis, litigation, education and advocacy to achieve racial, economic, and social justice for low-income immigrants.

National Immigration Law Center, "Legislative Priorities for Immigration Reform," January 2013. http://nilc.org.

Consider these questions as you read:

1. The essay opens with a personal anecdote about a couple who is caught up in a cross-border immigration limbo. Does this story make you sympathetic to illegal immigrants? Why or why not?
2. How convincing is the argument that allowing illegal immigrants a way to become citizens makes economic sense for the United States? Support your answer.
3. The essay ends by paraphrasing the quote that appears on the Statue of Liberty. Do you think those words remain important to the United States as a country? Why or why not?

Editor's note: The discussion that follows presents common arguments made in support of this perspective, reinforced by facts, quotes, and examples taken from various sources.

Emily Bonderer Cruz is American, and her husband is Mexican. Because he was deported for being in the United States illegally, her husband must live outside the United States for ten years before he can apply for citizenship. To be together, they live in the Mexican town of Ciudad Juárez, on the other side of the border from El Paso, Texas. Cruz works across the border in El Paso, where she makes a decent income—much more than what her husband earns working in a maquiladora, or factory, in Mexico. Cruz estimates that her husband makes about eighty cents an hour at his job. Sometimes it takes Cruz two hours to cross the border, so she usually leaves for work two hours before starting time.

Cruz's blog, *The Real Housewife of Ciudad Juárez*, is filled with tales, both mundane and harrowing, about attempting to stay married and wait out the ten years while living in a city that has been described by some as the murder capital of the world. Her story, along with countless other tales involving illegal immigrants, is just one of many that illustrate the need for reform. The United States should allow illegal immigrants who have proven themselves worthy of citizenship, such as Cruz's husband, to find a more immediate way toward citizenship.

Deserving of Citizenship

Hardworking undocumented workers who have no criminal record should be allowed to earn their citizenship. By remaining steadily employed and paying taxes, some type of amnesty would allow millions of illegals a chance to be self-sufficient, come out of the shadows, and secure higher-paying jobs with more secure working conditions. This is the crux of recent proposals for immigration reform. One bill that passed in the US Senate but has yet to pass in the House of Representatives would grant amnesty to certain illegals already living in the United States and ease the way for many others to gain permanent residence. It also makes provisions for those who are unworthy, such as those convicted of drunk driving, gang activity, passport fraud, domestic violence, or identity theft, to be banned from gaining citizenship.

Most Americans support a path to citizenship. According to Arizona senator John McCain, "Every poll I have seen, and I have seen hundreds, shows well over 70% of the American people support a path to citizenship. . . . They support a path to citizenship because they realize this is an issue of 11 million people who are living shadows, who are deprived of their rights as citizens and can't live normal lives and are not going back to where they came from."[23]

No one is more deserving of a path to citizenship than children who entered this country illegally with their families and have grown up, gone to school, and even attended college in the United States. These young people (known as DREAMers) have few or no ties to their countries of origin—and many speak only English. And yet hundreds have been deported to Mexico and other countries. This is inhumane. These young people must be allowed to begin the citizenship application process immediately.

> "[Americans] support a path to citizenship because they realize this is an issue of 11 million people who are living shadows, who are deprived of their rights as citizens and can't live normal lives and are not going back to where they came from."[23]
>
> —Arizona senator John McCain.

A Humane Answer

Immigration reform that offers people a chance to become fully participating US citizens makes sense on many levels, but most importantly it is the only humane answer to the problems associated with illegal immigration. Currently, illegals are not protected by US laws, even though they may have lived here for years and are contributing members of society. Without the protection of citizenship, illegals live a virtual second-class existence. Although they put into the system through Social Security and employment taxes, they are unable to reap the benefits of doing so. They must always be afraid, looking over their shoulder for a boss or a coworker who might turn them in to immigration authorities.

No one is served when these immigrants are deported, leaving their families broken and, sometimes, their children abandoned. As New York City mayor Michael Bloomberg said in a 2006 Senate hearing on immigration, the social consequences of deportation are devastating:

Let me ask you: Would we really want to spend billions of dollars on a round-up and deportation program that would split families in two—only to have these very same people and millions more, illegally enter our country again? Of course not. America is better than that—and smarter than that. There is only one practical solution, and it is a solution that respects the history of our nation: Offer those already here the opportunity to earn permanent status and keep their families together.[24]

Some critics argue that lax enforcement of the border has led to the situation we have now, and that awarding any sort of amnesty rewards illegal immigration. This claim, however, is simply untrue. Enforcement measures have increased in recent years—and they simply have not worked. For illegals, the pull of a better life is much stronger than the risk of deportation. As Alex Nowrasteh, an immigration policy analyst at the Cato Institute, writes: "Since 1933, the federal government has deported over 5.5 million people. Twenty-nine percent of those deportations, or 1.5 million, occurred during the first term of the Obama administration. George W. Bush's two full terms netted just over 2 million deportations, or 36 percent of all deportations since 1933."[25] No amount of expensive border measures can prevent illegal immigration, and using US resources to do so is a clear waste of money. According to the Center for American Progress, the US Border Patrol's annual budget has increased by 714 percent since 1992 along the US-Mexico border, yet each year more immigrants enter the country illegally.

Just Wait Your Turn?

Americans have to face facts when it comes to their southern border: it is economically advantageous and geographically possible to enter the United States illegally. To wait, possibly for years, to be chosen for legal status does not seem a realistic option to those who live south of the border. The backlog to enter the United States is simply too long and too onerous. As *New York Times* writer Julia Preston says,

> Because of numerical caps on visas for foreigners seeking residency, more than four million people who have been approved

Legal Status for Undocumented Immigrants Would Be Beneficial

Concerns about granting legal status to undocumented immigrants often turn on fears of harming the economy and taking jobs from US citizens. According to a 2013 Pew Research Center/*USA Today* poll, three-fourths of Americans believe that granting legal status—which could include a path to citizenship—to undocumented immigrants would help the economy. According to the poll, this is far more than the number who say such an action would hurt the economy and threaten jobs for citizens.

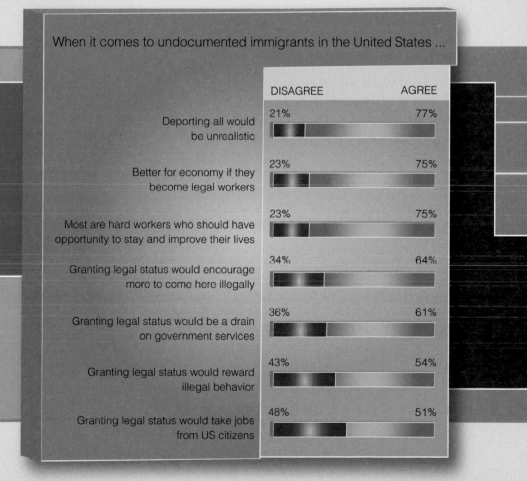

When it comes to undocumented immigrants in the United States ...

	DISAGREE	AGREE
Deporting all would be unrealistic	21%	77%
Better for economy if they become legal workers	23%	75%
Most are hard workers who should have opportunity to stay and improve their lives	23%	75%
Granting legal status would encourage more to come here illegally	34%	64%
Granting legal status would be a drain on government services	36%	61%
Granting legal status would reward illegal behavior	43%	54%
Granting legal status would take jobs from US citizens	48%	51%

Source: Pew Research Center, "Immigration: Key Data Points from Pew Research," June 26, 2013. www.pewresearch.org.

for [work in the United States] are waiting in those lines for visas, according to official figures. They include about 1.3 million Mexicans, but only 47,250 visas are available for Mexicans each year, according to the State Department. Some Mexican-born children of American citizens must wait 20 years for visas."[26]

The United States must make it easier for deserving immigrants to enter this country legally. According to the IPC, "Because the number of new immigrants admitted each year is based on numbers set by Congress in 1990, those admissions fail to reflect the legitimate demands for family unification and changes in workforce needs that have occurred over the last twenty years."[27]

Lastly, America will need a pool of unskilled workers because the labor force is shrinking. An aging baby boomer population, coupled with decreasing birthrates in the United States, will create a deficit in working Americans, meaning the problem of too many immigrants will simply take care of itself. Dowell Myers, a professor in the School of Policy, Planning, and Development at the University of Southern California predicts that by 2015 the demand for workers will increase as baby boomers age. "I wouldn't be surprised if Arizona starts pleading for Mexican workers who can help them in their retirement homes. . . . The potential here is to totally reverse our attitudes toward Mexican immigration,"[28] says Myers.

For economic and moral reasons, then, the United States must once again, to paraphrase poet Emma Lazarus, open its arms to the tired, the poor, and the hungry masses yearning to breathe free.

> "There is only one practical solution, and it is a solution that respects the history of our nation: Offer those already here the opportunity to earn permanent status and keep their families together."[24]
>
> —Michael Bloomberg, the mayor of New York City.

Illegal Immigrants Should Not Be Offered a Path to Citizenship

> "I adamantly oppose offering citizenship to those here illegally. I firmly belief it is morally wrong to, in any way, reward illegal behavior."

—Laredo, Texas, businessman Gary Jacobs.

Quoted in Richard Finger, "Is Rule of Law Dead? Should We Reward Illegal Immigrants with Path to Citizenship?," *Forbes*, July 23, 2013. www.forbes.com.

Consider these questions as you read:

1. Fewer than half of eligible illegal immigrants sought citizenship under a 1986 amnesty law. Does this prove that people here illegally do not really want to become citizens? Why or why not?
2. Many people believe that amnesty rewards illegal behavior. What do you think?
3. Do you think that illegal immigrants who are granted citizenship are less likely to assimilate? Explain your answer.

Editor's note: The discussion that follows presents common arguments made in support of this perspective, reinforced by facts, quotes, and examples taken from various sources.

The hand wringing and misplaced empathy over the illegal immigration debate has got to stop. Illegal immigrants are lawbreakers, no matter how long they have managed to evade detection in the United States; no matter if they were able to bring children here and raise those children in the United States, effectively, without a country. The United States must maintain its borders, and it must deport individuals who do not obey its laws. With the country still in an economic recession, it seems ridiculous to talk about adding millions of people to the United States when 12.3 million Americans remain unemployed. The real reason behind amnesty is likely a far more sinister motive: whatever political entity or party allows millions to be granted citizenship allows millions to gain voting rights and guarantees virtual support in elections. Meanwhile, supporters of immigration reform work on Americans' guilt about the plight of illegals.

A Plan That Failed Before

There is nothing new about trying to make illegals legal, in spite of the fact that it does not work and creates more problems for the United States. The United States tried this before, with the 1986 Amnesty Act. Then, 2.7 million immigrants were legalized simply by paying a fine, learning English, and having a residency requirement. Once these caveats were met, illegals could become full citizens. The lessons learned with that act need to be remembered: The process was too long, expensive, and complicated. Illegals could not afford the fees, and many did not speak English and so could not perform the necessary requirements to apply for amnesty. According to a 2010 survey by the DHS, only about 40 percent of the 2.7 million illegal immigrants who were granted green cards under the 1986 law went through the work and commitment to become citizens.

> "Half the people in '86 that could have gotten amnesty didn't apply. Many people don't want to be citizens of our country. . . . They want to come here, they want to work hard, they want to provide for their families. . . . Not necessarily all of them want to stay as citizens."[29]
>
> —Former Florida governor Jeb Bush.

This statistic illustrates better than most that illegals want to be able to sneak over the border and take advantage of the United States economically without taking on the obligations that come with citizenship. As former Florida governor Jeb Bush says, "Half the people in '86 that could have gotten amnesty didn't apply. Many people don't want to be citizens of our country. . . . They want to come here, they want to work hard, they want to provide for their families. . . . Not necessarily all of them want to stay as citizens."[29]

Making citizenship easier might create new problems that the United States is not prepared to face. The United States can learn from the experiences of other countries. In many instances, amnesty created major problems. In Spain in 2005, for example, the government thought three hundred thousand people would apply for amnesty when it was offered; eight hundred thousand showed up. Similar situations occurred in Italy and Belgium. No country can absorb that many immigrants. As Paul Belien, editor of the *Brussels Journal*, contends, "The European experience teaches us that governments always underestimate the number of people who can apply for an amnesty, and that amnesties do not close floodgates, they open them."[30]

Border Enforcement Works

Those who urge the federal government to offer citizenship to illegals often do so because they view border enforcement efforts as expensive, inefficient, and unworkable. This view conveniently ignores the fact that enhanced border enforcement is actually working. W. James Antle III, a contributing editor to the *American Conservative*, describes the progress that has been made in reducing illegal immigration:

> The investment in border security and interior enforcement has increased. There are more fences and border patrol agents. The government is now believed to have effective control of 57 percent of the U.S. border. While the sluggish American economy has caused many illegal immigrants to go home—the unemployment rate is now lower in Mexico than in the U.S.—improved enforcement is credited with about half the drop.[31]

Other measures to fix the border have also been working. Under the 2006 Secure Fence Act, former president George W. Bush envisioned 700 miles (1,127 km) of permanent border fencing along the US-Mexico border. That goal was never fully realized, but some counties erected their own border fences. Yuma, Arizona, for instance, reinforced its section of the border with three fences. Border Patrol agent Michael Ber-

Illegal immigrants granted amnesty would be eligible for many government services and benefits that they currently do not receive. These
include Social Security and Medicare. Full amnesty for all undocumented
households could cost US taxpayers billions of dollars each year. The
interim phase refers to the time period before amnesty recipients are
eligible to receive full government benefits.

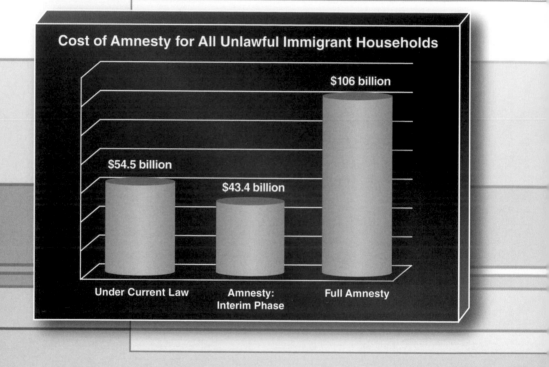

Cost of Amnesty for All Unlawful Immigrant Households

$106 billion

$54.5 billion

$43.4 billion

Under Current Law   Amnesty: Full Amnesty
Interim Phase

Source: Robert Rector and Jason Richwine, "The Fiscal Cost of Unlawful Immigrants and Amnesty to the US
Taxpayer," Heritage Foundation, May 6, 2013. www.heritage.org.

nacke argues that the triple fence resulted in a 72 percent decline in illegal immigrant apprehensions. If the United States had the political will
to reinforce the entire US-Mexico border as it has done in Yuma, illegal
immigration would be greatly curtailed.

Just as the United States has lacked the political will to build a strong
border fence, it also has failed to follow through with other measures,

such as employer sanctions for hiring illegal immigrants. Though the 1986 Immigration Reform and Control Act required employers to verify workers' eligibility to work legally and made it illegal for employers to knowingly hire unauthorized immigrants, employers are rarely held accountable. The Border Patrol regularly does sweeps in which illegals are rounded up and deported, but few employers are criminally punished. Most employers face a fine and a slap on the wrist. Criminally prosecuting employers would go a long way to curtailing illegal immigration.

Had any of these enforcement measures been carried out as intended, the issue of rewarding lawbreakers with the privilege of citizenship would be moot. As it now stands, however, the United States is yet again considering such action.

> "The European experience teaches us that governments always underestimate the number of people who can apply for an amnesty, and that amnesties do not close floodgates, they open them."[30]
>
> —Paul Belien, editor of the *Brussels Journal*.

Whose Morality?

Amnesty condones and rewards illegal behavior and is unfair to those who follow the grueling regulatory requirements to become a citizen. Many legal immigrants agree that amnesty is a mistake. Alex Khazanovich, a recent immigrant from Russia who is now a US citizen, contends that "it is just wrong to disregard when people do something that is against the law. . . . We don't want to reward those who figured they will bypass the process that is in place."[32]

It is not just immigrants who oppose amnesty. American citizens are also offended by the message it gives. Laredo businessman Gary Jacobs explains:

I adamantly oppose offering citizenship to those here illegally. I firmly believe it is morally wrong to, in any way, reward illegal behavior. It undermines our rule of law. . . . I am for offering most of the people working here illegally resident alien work permits with time restrictions that can be reviewed, but if they want a path to citizenship (to be able to vote), they need to start at the back of the line and gain entry by legal means.[33]

The citizenship process, then, should be upheld as an important part of becoming an American. Those not fortunate enough to be US citizens by birth should be required to work for this privilege; one must earn the right to be called an American by learning the country's laws and by formally pledging loyalty to uphold them. Becoming a citizen of the United States should be more than just a white flag of surrender because someone entered the country illegally and managed to avoid getting caught. A person granted amnesty would have far less attachment, and far less reason to assimilate, then those that go through the formal citizenship process. As *Forbes* writer Richard Finger puts it,

> A lot of people, me included, rightly or wrongly, are concerned about assimilation. America by so many metrics, especially economic, is the greatest civilization ever created. I think there is fear that if undocumented aliens, and not just Mexicans, are granted citizenship, that they will not adopt the American culture. There is anxiety that people arrive on our shores for the generous benefits programs. America has always been the great melting pot where for the past two hundred plus years people from everywhere, including Mexico, have arrived, learned English, and adopted the American ethos. It is this great American ethos that inexorably weaves our population together, and causes Americans to stand strong in times of crisis. Some are afraid the wholesale rewarding of citizenship erodes the American fabric.[34]

For economic and moral reasons, illegal immigrants need to be sent a strong message that bypassing US laws is not what it takes to remain in this country. And it is not the way to obtain citizenship.

Chapter Four

How Should Immigration Laws Be Enforced?

State and Local Authorities Should Enforce Immigration Laws

- States already have the resources, such as local police, to enforce immigration law.
- New laws that militarize the border endanger citizens on both sides of the fence.
- States that are overburdened with illegal immigration can place more of a priority on arresting and deporting illegal aliens.

The Debate at a Glance

National Authorities Should Enforce Immigration Laws

- The federal government is the only entity that can consistently enforce immigration law across all fifty states.
- Using local law enforcement to enforce immigration law causes distrust between the police and immigrants.
- The federal government already has the laws in place to enforce immigration law.

State and Local Authorities Should Enforce Immigration Laws

"In light of the predominance of federal immigration restrictions in modern times, it is easy to lose sight of the States' traditional role in regulating immigration—and to overlook their sovereign prerogative to do so."

—Antonin Scalia, Justice of the US Supreme Court.

Antonin Scalia, dissenting opinion, *Arizona et al. v. United States,* 567 U.S. (2012). http://s3 .documentcloud.org.

Consider these questions as you read:

1. Some argue that local police should enforce immigration laws because they routinely have more contact with illegals, but others contend that this would make illegal immigrants less likely to report crimes. Which is the most convincing argument? Why?
2. What evidence does the author give to argue that the Border Patrol is more likely to use lethal force? Given what you know about local police, do you think the author is accurate in saying that the Border Patrol is more likely to use lethal force? Explain your answer.
3. The author thinks that the states can enforce immigration law better than the federal government because they can devote enough resources to meet their illegal immigration problem. Do you agree? Why or why not?

Editor's note: The discussion that follows presents common arguments made in support of this perspective, reinforced by facts, quotes, and examples taken from various sources.

The federal government has failed to effectively control illegal immigration. States can no longer rely on the federal government for this. It is time that states be given the resources to do the difficult job the federal government will not or cannot do. State and local police are needed to do the job. According to NumbersUSA, an organization that advocates measures to reduce immigration,

> State and local police are badly needed to help overwhelmed federal immigration authorities apprehend and detain illegal aliens in the interior of our country. Illegal aliens outnumber Immigration and Customs Enforcement (ICE) agents by over 5,000 to one. Only about 5,000 ICE agents are responsible for enforcing the immigration laws in the interior of our country. This number is too small to apprehend more than a fraction of the illegal alien population now here.[35]

The Benefits of a Bigger Workforce

The states can help with this problem. They already have local law enforcement officers who encounter illegals every day. Local police and highway patrol stop illegals for traffic violations and other infractions in the normal course of their day. There is no reason why they should not have the ability to arrest illegal immigrants and begin the process of deportation.

State and local police make up approximately 96 percent of law enforcement personnel nationwide. Distributed over this wide number of officers, immigration enforcement would become a small duty for a large number rather than a huge duty for a few. As NumbersUSA claims, "Were these state and local police officers to detain and turn over to ICE every illegal alien with whom they come into contact during the normal course of their duties, hundreds of thousands more illegal aliens could be removed from the United States each year."[36]

Additionally, civilian border patrols could assist local police and fill holes in national security. Organizations such as the Minuteman Civil Defense Corps, made up of civilians, are already active in border towns in Arizona. On a national scale, these groups could provide a valuable service, becoming the eyes and ears for law enforcement. According to Minuteman founder Chris Simcox,

> It is now more important than ever for citizens to rise to the occasion and fill a void in National security. Minuteman Civil Defense Corps . . . volunteers will now patrol the border with over 100 fully armed Citizens who consider themselves members of the unorganized state militia; we have the legal right and moral obligation as per our Arizona State Constitution and Federal Constitution and our respect for American citizens. Our intent is to send a strong message to the world that we will stand defiant to invaders and protect the borders of our country.[37]

Local civilian patrols make sense. In areas such as Arizona, where citizens are most affected by illegal immigration, there are most likely more volunteers eager to help secure their homes and families against the torrent of illegal immigration.

A Militarized Border

Not only is the federal government hopelessly overwhelmed by immigration enforcement, but the method by which it controls the border also is wrongheaded. Militarizing the border with the military and National Guard is simply not the way to police the border. It essentially militarizes the US-Mexico border, which sets a dangerous precedent. Before becoming US secretary of defense, Chuck Hagel was a senator from Nebraska. While a senator, Hagel commented,

> I think we have to be very careful here. That's not the role of our military. That's not the role of our national guard. . . . Let's start with the fact do we even have the capacity? . . . We've got national guard members on their second, third and fourth tours in Iraq. We have stretched our military as thin as we have ever seen it in modern times. And what in the world are we talking about here,

sending a national guard that we may not have any capacity to send up to—or down to—protect borders? That's not their role.[38]

This is overkill. Mexico is, after all, an ally—an ally that it is in the United States's interest to keep. As Christina Parker, a member of the group Border Network for Human Rights, contends, "Immigration reform does not mean more drones, more walls, more helicopters or checks to the Department of Defense and military contractors. . . . We are the only place in the world where we are militarizing the border between two allied countries that are not even in conflict."[39]

Unnecessary Lethal Force

The US Border Patrol, whose primary job is policing the borders, is being asked to do too much. In addition to apprehending and detaining people who enter the country illegally, Border Patrol agents are involved in efforts to fight drug trafficking and even terrorism. Even when performing its primary duties, the Border Patrol has faltered badly. Since 2010 there have been six fatal shootings on Mexican soil by US agents, prompting formal complaints by the Mexican government about unnecessary use of lethal force and heightening tensions between the two countries. In one of these fatal shootings, which occurred in September 2012, Guillermo Arévalo Pedroza was shot and killed by a Border Patrol agent while picnicking with his wife and two young girls on the Mexican side of the Rio Grande near Laredo, Texas. He died in the arms of his nine-year-old daughter. A similar incident happened in October 2012, when a sixteen-year-old boy was shot when Border Patrol agents fired over the border at retreating men they thought were drug traffickers.

"Were these state and local police officers to detain and turn over to ICE every illegal alien with whom they come into contact during the normal course of their duties, hundreds of thousands more illegal aliens could be removed from the United States each year."[36]

—NumbersUSA, an organization that advocates measures to reduce immigration.

57

State Laws Requiring Verification of Legal Status for Public Benefits Are Effective

Many states have enacted legislation to deal with the financial burdens posed when illegal immigrants use public services for which they are not eligible. One type of legislation requires applicants to verify their legal status—beyond what is mandated by the federal governement—in order to receive benefits provided by the state. These laws effectively prevent the illegal use of public services.

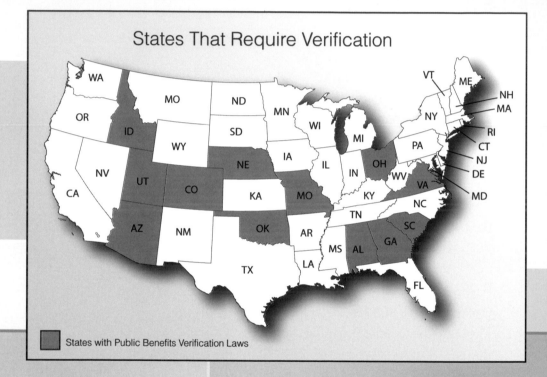

States That Require Verification

States with Public Benefits Verification Laws

Source: National Immigration Law Center, "State Immigration-Related Legislation: Last Year's Key Battles Set the Stage for 2012," January 2012. www.nilc.org.

One of the problems is that the Border Patrol consists mostly of former members of the military, who are trained to shoot first and ask questions later. State and local police, on the other hand, are trained in negotiation techniques and, especially, on use of force in places where civilians are present. These are among the reasons that state and local governments are the better choice for dealing with illegal immigrants.

States Already Enforce Immigration Laws

Dozens of states have already taken on immigration enforcement responsibilities. Like Arizona, Alabama allows police to detain possible illegal immigrants and also makes it a crime for illegals to conduct business in the state. Republican senator Scott Beason commented on the law: "I think we did what we intended to do. . . . We did see apparently thousands of illegal aliens leave the state. It did open up jobs for a number of Alabamians, which was really our main goal."[40]

State laws such as Alabama's are much more effective because they are applied on a local level and are staffed by local law enforcement officers who have a stake in their communities. As Kansas secretary of state Kris W. Kobach, who supports strong immigration laws at the state level, contends, "If state and local government can add their shoulders to the wheel and help to increase the total amount of enforcement . . . that will change the cost-benefit analysis of your typical illegal alien who says, 'You know what, it's getting harder for me to work illegally in the United States. It's getting harder for me to get these public benefits, and I'm going home.'"[41]

States also have a stake in reducing the burden that illegal immigrants place on the social services they offer. If health clinics were able to check citizenship status and call local authorities, for example, these clinics would be more available for citizens. In addition, clinics are never reimbursed by the federal government for the care they give illegals. As Randy Brinson, a doctor at Jackson Hospital in Montgomery, Alabama, explains, "When they come to the emergency room, we don't check their immigration status, we just know it's someone who is sick. So the reality is they come in, we take care of them, and we very rarely get compensated for their care."[42]

> "If state and local government can add their shoulders to the wheel and help to increase the total amount of enforcement . . . that will change the cost-benefit analysis of your typical illegal alien who says, 'You know what, it's getting harder for me to work illegally in the United States. It's getting harder for me to get these public benefits, and I'm going home.'"[41]
>
> —Kansas secretary of state Kris W. Kobach.

Finally, the burden of illegal immigration affects some states, such as California, Arizona, and Texas, much more than others. These states, then, can choose to devote more of their resources to making sure taxpayers are not paying for illegals to use state services. Ira Mehlman, the spokesman for FAIR, explains:

> When the federal government fails to enforce our immigration laws, it is the taxpayers in Arizona, or Maryland, or whatever state you happen to be living in who are then forced to pay for education, for healthcare, for other social services. They're the ones who have to deal with crime that may be associated with illegal immigration. These burdens are felt at the state and local level.[43]

It is a well-known axiom that government works best when it is at the local level. It is time to give the responsibility for immigration control to state and local governments.

National Authorities Should Enforce Immigration Laws

"[Immigration] laws must be enforced, like desegregation laws, by the Federal government."

—Michael Bargo Jr., a writer for the magazine *American Thinker*.

Michael Bargo Jr., "Federal Enforcement, Not Immigration Reform, Is Needed," *American Thinker*, May 4, 2013. www.americanthinker.com.

Consider these questions as you read:

1. What evidence is given to prove that enforcement of immigration law and local law enforcement must remain separate? Do you agree with this evidence? Why or why not?
2. The essay argues that local police will not be familiar with immigration laws and will violate immigrants' rights. What do you think?
3. Several examples of underused immigration policies that could help the federal government improve its immigration enforcement are presented here. On reading this essay and the previous one, do you agree that this would help end the debate over which entity should enforce immigration law? Why or why not?

Editor's note: The discussion that follows presents common arguments made in support of this perspective, reinforced by facts, quotes, and examples taken from various sources.

On the whole, the states do a great job of dealing with local crime. But they should not have control over issues that are clearly in the federal domain. When states get involved in federal policy, the result is often chaos. This can be seen in issues such as the legalization of marijuana. Once states were allowed to pass their own laws governing a substance considered to be illegal under federal law, enforcement efforts immediately began to suffer.

The same will likely occur if state and local entities are given responsibility for enforcing federal immigration policies, especially with regard to illegal immigrants. It is by design that states have only a limited role to play in this area. The courts have ruled that the US Constitution leaves immigration policy to the federal government. According to the Congressional Research Service's 2012 report to Congress,

> The power to prescribe rules as to which aliens may enter the United States and which aliens may be removed resides solely with the federal government, and primarily with Congress. Concomitant to its exclusive power to determine which aliens may enter and which may stay in the country, the federal government also has the power to proscribe activities that subvert this system.[44]

Mistrust of Police

When states take immigration law into their own hands, there are often unintended consequences. Currently, local police are trusted members of the community, and citizens and noncitizens can turn to them when they have been victimized by a crime. Transferring the role of immigration control to local law enforcement would undermine the trust and cooperation that exists between local police and illegal immigrant communities. People who are in this country illegally would begin to avoid police contact for fear that they or family members would be subject to immigration enforcement. According to San Francisco district attorney George Gascon, who has previously served as the chief of police in San Francisco and in Mesa, Arizona, "In the absence of federal action, states have taken immigration law into their own hands, implementing laws that drive a wedge between law enforcement and the people we are sworn to serve."[45]

"The power to prescribe rules as to which aliens may enter the United States and which aliens may be removed resides solely with the federal government."[44]

—Congressional Research Service, 2012 report to Congress.

62

A 2013 study by the think tank Policy Link found that immigrants, both legal and illegal, are already socially isolated and mistrustful of the police. In a survey of 2,004 Latinos in Los Angeles, Houston, Chicago, and Phoenix, about 44 percent of the respondents who are US citizens or permanent residents said that they would be unlikely to report a crime to the local police. The figure jumped to 70 percent among illegals asked the same question.

Nik Theodore of the Department of Urban Planning and Policy at the University of Illinois at Chicago directly attributes the lack of trust to the fact that state and local law enforcement authorities have become increasingly involved in immigration enforcement:

> An important unintended consequence of police involvement in immigration enforcement [is] a substantial portion of the Latino populations in Cook, Harris, Los Angeles, and Maricopa Counties are reluctant to voluntarily contact the police to report a crime or to provide information about crimes, specifically because they fear that police officers will inquire about the immigration status of themselves, their friends, or their family members.[46]

Distrust Will Mean More Crime Against Immigrants

This distrust will only worsen if states take on a larger enforcement role. The Policy Link study "confirms what police experts have been saying for decades,"[47] contends Thomas A. Saenz, the president and general counsel for the Mexican American Legal Defense and Educational Fund, a Latino nonprofit civil rights organization headquartered in Los Angeles. The results of this study prove that there must be a clear distinction between local law enforcement and immigration enforcement. Otherwise the United States will have a desperate underclass that will be easily victimized by criminals who know these crimes will not be punished.

In addition, local police are ill equipped for this because they remain unskilled in enforcing immigration law. The immigration status of a specific person can vary greatly according to complex federal immigration regulations and would be very difficult for the average police officer to determine. Cities where illegal immigration is significant are cities where police departments are already overwhelmed simply fighting crime. Learning immigration law and then enforcing it would be an unrealistic responsibility to add.

This lack of understanding of immigration law can lead to abuse of immigrants. Alabama's immigration law is a good example of this abuse of power. The law not only calls for police to detain suspects on a reasonable suspicion that they are in the country illegally but also allows illegals to be prosecuted if they are conducting any sort of business. This broad and unreasonable law has made illegals afraid to exercise their rights under the new laws. For example, eighteen-year-old Maria Lola Melisio dropped out of high school in the eleventh grade because her mother thought the new Alabama law would call into question her daughter's status and that she might be deported. Now, in order to apply for legal status under the Deferred Action for Childhood Arrivals program, Melisio needs a high school diploma—an impossible situation. The Border Patrol would at least be familiar with new laws and enforce them fairly.

Haphazard State Laws

State immigration law can also interfere with needed immigrant labor. In the summer of 2011, for example, a tough new immigration law in Georgia produced an agriculture labor shortage during peak harvest season. Without the necessary laborers to harvest their crops, state farmers watched millions of dollars' worth of blueberries, onions, and other crops rot in their fields.

Instead of haphazard and unfair state laws, the federal government must step up its enforcement of immigration law using tools that are already at its disposal, such as making E-Verify (a program that allows employers to verify a prospective employee's immigration status) mandatory across all states. As immigration writer Michael Bargo Jr. contends, "What the American people need to understand is that statutory improvements are not what is needed to correct the illegal immigration problem. What is needed is Federal enforcement of laws, whether current or future laws."[48] As Bargo and others understand, federal programs work. There is no need for further laws or state involvement.

Federal Enforcement Has Slowed Unauthorized Immigration

The federal government spends millions of dollars each year to fund programs aimed at decreasing illegal immigration. Data from population surveys shows that unauthorized immigration is decreasing as spending has increased, a clear sign that federal enforcement of immigration laws is working.

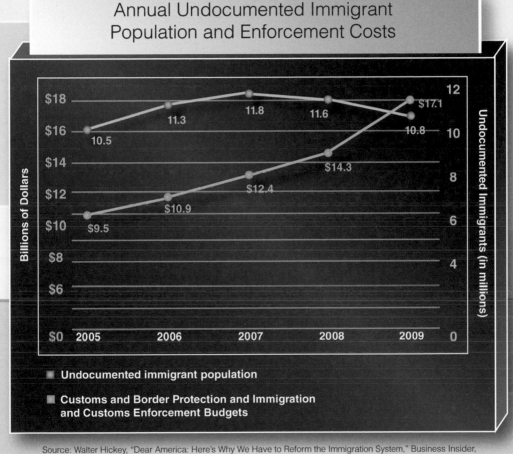

Annual Undocumented Immigrant Population and Enforcement Costs

Billions of Dollars

$18
$16
$14
$12
$10
$8
$6
$0

10.5   11.3   11.8   11.6   10.8
$9.5 $10.9 $12.4 $14.3 $17.1

2005   2006   2007   2008   2009

Undocumented Immigrants (in millions)

12   10   8   6   4   0

■ Undocumented immigrant population

■ Customs and Border Protection and Immigration and Customs Enforcement Budgets

Source: Walter Hickey, "Dear America: Here's Why We Have to Reform the Immigration System," Business Insider, May 3, 2013. www.businessinsider.com.

The Secure Fence Act

One federal mandate that has been consistently overlooked, for example, is the Secure Fence Act of 2006. The act delegated federal funds to build a secure fence along the southern border of the United States. In signing the act, George W. Bush said, "This bill will make our borders more secure. It is an important step toward immigration reform."[49]

An enhanced border fence would greatly aid the federal government in enforcing immigration law. The organization Let Freedom Ring states the reasons for a federally funded border fence on its website, including that the fence would help ensure national security in several ways. For example, the fence would protect against terrorists who could bring small weaponry, including small, nuclear, suitcase weapons, into the country. The border is so important that the fence needs to be manned by a military force to make sure that both those who want to do harm to US citizens and those illegals who refuse to obey the laws of the United States are no longer allowed to freely cross the border.

> "I urge the immediate deployment of U.S. military troops and equipment on our borders to seal them against those who would cause us harm."[50]
>
> —Former Border Patrol agent David Stoddard.

Beefing up already existing laws would mean the American public would regain its confidence that the federal government can take care of the immigration issue without state interference. According to former Border Patrol agent David Stoddard,

> The U.S. Border Patrol simply cannot handle its mission under present restraints. Its job is to protect the American public and preserve the sanctity of our international borders. That cannot be accomplished while our borders are over run by aliens of every nationality and while bureaucrats place unreasonable restrictions on how agents operate. I urge the immediate deployment of U.S. military troops and equipment on our borders to seal them against those who would cause us harm. This could be only a temporary measure to allow us to regain control to again become a sovereign nation.[50]

The United States needs the political will and determination to enforce its border laws. Federal oversight allows for all citizens and noncitizens of this country to be treated equally, under the same laws. That is what the Constitution of this nation demands.

Source Notes

Overview: Illegal Immigration

1. Quoted in *30 Days*, "Immigration," FX channel (season 2, episode 1), July 26, 2006.
2. Jeffrey S. Passel and D'Vera Cohn, "U.S. Unauthorized Immigration Flows Are Down Sharply Since Mid-Decade," Pew Research Center, Hispanic Trends Project, September 10, 2010. www.pewhispanic.org.
3. Jeffrey S. Passel, D'Vera Cohn, and Ana Gonzalez-Barrera, "Population Decline of Unauthorized Immigrants Stalls, May Have Reversed," Pew Research Center, Hispanic Trends Project, September 23, 2013. www.pewhispanic.org.

Chapter One: How Does Illegal Immigration Affect the Economy?

4. Federation for American Immigration Reform, "Illegal Aliens Taking U.S. Jobs (2013)," March 2013. www.fairus.org.
5. Quoted in Fox News, "Welfare Tab for Children of Illegal Immigrants Estimated at $600M in L.A. County," January 19, 2011. www.foxnews.com.
6. Colorado Alliance for Immigration Reform, "Economic Costs of Legal and Illegal Immigration." www.cairco.org.
7. Quoted in Alison St. John, "Costs and Benefits of Illegal Immigration Are Unequally Distributed," KPBS, July 23, 2010. www.kpbs.org.
8. Eduardo Porter, "Immigration and American Jobs," *New York Times*, October 19, 2012. www.nytimes.com.
9. Francine J. Lipman, "Taxing Undocumented Immigrants: Separate, Unequal, and Without Representation," *Harvard Latino Law Review*, Spring 2006. http://harvardllr.com.
10. Adam Davidson, "Do Illegal Immigrants Actually Hurt the U.S. Economy?," *New York Times*, February 12, 2013. www.nytimes.com.

Chapter Two: How Does Illegal Immigration Impact America's Safety and Security?

11. US Department of Justice, "National Drug Intelligence Center Releases *National Drug Threat Assessment* 2010," Office of Public Affairs, March 25, 2010. www.justice.gov.

12. Roger D. McGrath, "Double Down: Illegal Aliens and Crime," *Chronicles*, July 12, 2010. www.chroniclesmagazine.org.

13. Quoted in Terence P. Jeffrey, "Justice Department: Border Patrol Agents Assaulted Daily, Kidnappings Every 35 Hours in Phoenix, 1 in 5 Teens Using Drugs Predominantly Supplied by Mexican Traffickers," CNSNews.com, April 28, 2010. http://cnsnews.com.

14. Quoted in Edwin Mora, "663 Illegal Aliens from Countries with Ties to Terrorism Arrested Along Southwest Border in 2010, Senator Says," CNSNews.com, March 18, 2011. http://cnsnews.com.

15. US House Committee on Homeland Security, Subcommittee on Oversight, Investigations, and Management, "A Line in the Sand: Countering Crime, Violence, and Terror at the Southwest Border," November 2012. http://mccaul.house.gov.

16. Quoted in Radley Balko, "The El Paso Miracle," *Reason*, July 6, 2009. http://reason.com.

17. Quoted in Tom Barry, "The Truth About Illegal Immigration and Crime: Immigrants, Whether Legal or Illegal, Are Substantially Less Likely to Commit Crimes or to Be Incarcerated than U.S. Citizens," *Hunger Notes*, 2008. www.worldhunger.org.

18. Daniel Griswold, "Unfounded Fear of Immigrant Crime Grips Arizona," *Washington Times,* May 25, 2010. www.cato.org.

19. Quoted in Dennis Wagner, "Violence Is Not Up on Arizona Border Despite Mexican Drug War," *Arizona Republic*, May 2, 2010. www.azcentral.com.

20. Spencer S. Hsu, "U.S. Police Chiefs Say Arizona Immigration Law Will Increase Crime," *Washington Post*, May 27, 2010. www.washingtonpost.com.

21. Jason Arvak, "Arizona Immigration Law Increases Crime," Moderate Voice, May 26, 2010. http://themoderatevoice.com.

22. American Immigration Law Foundation, "Immigrants Aren't Undermining Our Nation's Security; Flawed Immigration Laws Are," 2008. www.ailf.org.

Chapter Three: Should Illegal Immigrants Be Offered a Path to Citizenship?

23. Quoted in Mike Hall, "McCain: Path to Citizenship Must Be 'Fundamental Element' of Immigration Reform," AFL-CIO, July 30, 2013. www.aflcio.org.

24. Quoted in US Senate Committee on the Judiciary, "Testimony of the Honorable Michael R. Bloomberg," July 5, 2006. www.judiciary.senate.gov.

25. Alex Nowrasteh, "SAFE Act an Expensive Boondoggle," Cato Institute, August 7, 2013. www.cato.org.

26. Julia Preston, "Path to Citizenship Divides Congress and, Polls Show, Confuses Country," *New York Times*, April 4, 2013. www.nytimes.com.

27. Immigration Policy Center, "Tackling the Toughest Questions on Immigration Reform," July 29, 2013. www.immigrationpolicy.org.

28. Quoted in Arian Campo-Flores, "Don't Fence Them In," Daily Beast, May 27, 2010. www.thedailybeast.com.

29. Quoted in Jordan Fabian, "Jeb Bush: No Path to Citizenship in Immigration Reform," ABC News, March 4, 2013. http://abcnews.go.com.

30. Paul Belien, "Let's Not Go Dutch," *American Conservative*, August 27, 2007. www.theamericanconservative.com.

31. W. James Antle III, "How Not to Fix Immigration," *American Conservative*, February 5, 2013. www.theamericanconservative.com.

32. Quoted in Jude Joffe-Block, "Not All Immigrants Agree on Offering Others 'a Path to Citizenship,'" PRI's the World, June 27, 2013. www.theworld.org.

33. Quoted in Richard Finger, "Is Rule of Law Dead? Should We Reward Illegal Immigrants with Path to Citizenship?," *Forbes*, July 23, 2013. www.forbes.com.

34. Finger, "Is Rule of Law Dead? Should We Reward Illegal Immigrants with Path to Citizenship?"

Chapter Four: How Should Immigration Laws Be Enforced?

35. NumbersUSA, "The Need for State and Local Immigration Law Enforcement of Immigration Laws," March 27, 2008. www.numbersusa.com.

36. NumbersUSA, "The Need for State and Local Immigration Law Enforcement of Immigration Laws."

37. Chris Simcox, "Simcox Manifesto," American Patrol Report. www.americanpatrol.com.

38. Quoted in ABC News, "This Week with George Stephanopoulos," May 14, 2006. http://abcnews.go.com.

39. Quoted in Lorena Figueroa, "Protesting Border 'Militarization': 250 in El Paso March Against Surge in Immigration Reform Bill," *El Paso Times*, July 18, 2013. www.elpasotimes.com.

40. Quoted in Debbie Elliott, "Federal-State Tug of War: Drawing the Lines in Immigration Overhaul," NPR, December 17, 2012. www.npr.org.

41. Quoted in Elliott, "Federal-State Tug of War."

42. Quoted in Elliott, "Federal-State Tug of War."

43. Quoted in David A. Patten, "Arizona-Style Rebellions over Immigration Spread," *Newsmax*, May 5, 2010. www.newsmax.com.

44. Michael John Garcia and Kate M. Manuel, *Authority of State and Local Police to Enforce Federal Immigration Law*, Congressional Research Service, September 10, 2012. www.fas.org.

45. George Gascon, "Why Cops Should Back Immigration Reform," CNN, June 19, 2013. www.cnn.com.

46. Nik Theodore, "Insecure Communities: Latino Perceptions of Police Involvement in Immigration Enforcement," Department of Urban Planning and Policy, University of Illinois at Chicago, May 2013. www.uic.edu.

47. Quoted in Brian Bennett, "Latinos Now Less Likely to Report Crimes to Police, Poll Says," *Los Angeles Times*, May 7, 2013. www.latimes.com.

48. Michael Bargo Jr., "Federal Enforcement, Not Immigration Reform, Is Needed," *American Thinker*, May 4, 2013. www.americanthinker.com.

49. Quoted in White House, "President Bush Signs Secure Fence Act," October 26, 2006. http://georgewbush-whitehouse.archives.gov.

50. Quoted in ProCon.org, "Should the US Military Patrol the Borders?," February 5, 2009. Immigration.procon.org.

Illegal Immigration Facts

Demographics

- According to the IPC, nearly half of all long-term illegal immigrants are homeowners, and more than three-fifths of illegal immigrants have resided in the United States for more than ten years.
- Approximately 4.5 million native-born children have at least one parent who is not authorized to reside in the United States.
- According to the group Immigration Works USA, more than half of all illegal immigrants between the ages of twenty-five and sixty-four have at least a high school diploma.
- Close to half of all adult illegal aliens live in homes with children under the age of eighteen, according to the Hispanic Trends Project of the Pew Research Center (formerly the Pew Hispanic Center).

Illegal Immigration and the Economy

- According to a 2013 Heritage Foundation report, proposed immigration reform legislation, if passed, will cost taxpayers $6.3 trillion to implement.
- According to Giovanni Peri, an economist at the University of California, Davis, illegal workers complement skilled laborers by taking on routine tasks so that skilled workers can concentrate on their higher-level jobs. In states with high immigration levels, skilled workers made more money and worked more hours.
- In early 2013 dairy farmers from western and central New York issued a statement saying that they were suffering from labor shortages because of increased scrutiny by immigration authorities.
- A study published in July 2013 in the *American Sociological Review* suggests that Mexican men are less likely to cross the US-Mexico border if they believe they can find a job in their native country.

Legal Issues

- Undocumented immigrants, including unattended children, who have been taken into custody and face deportation are not entitled to public defenders.
- A 2012 study by the Vera Institute of Justice showed that approximately 40 percent of undocumented children in custody may qualify for statuses that make them exemption from deportation.

- A bill being debated in the California legislature would limit the role of state and local police in enforcing penalties for immigration violations.
- According to an April 22, 2013 *Washington Times* article, the Obama administration has approved 99.5 percent of applications of those who have applied for legal status under the nondeportation policy for young adults, which translates to legal status for more than 250,000 formerly illegal immigrants.

Immigration Reform

- Key supporters of immigration reform are calling for legislation that would require all employers to verify the legal immigration status of all new employees using a photo-matching system. Companies would have five years to comply.
- Approximately 75 percent of visas are issued to immigrants on the basis of their family ties in America. If a merit program is implemented, closer to 50 percent of visas would go to family members of immigrants who already reside in the country. One proposed solution to immigration reform is the creation of two new guest-worker programs: one specifically for farmworkers and one for low-wage workers.
- Spokespersons for the group United We Dream, an organization of undocumented youths, has stated that although it supports the proposed five-year path to citizenship for young people, the path for older illegal immigrants—approximately thirteen years—is far too long.
- Proposed reforms include raising the cap on high-skilled visas, which would give employers in the technology and science fields tens of thousands of new employees.

The US-Mexico Border

- A group called No More Deaths makes camp approximately 10 miles (16 km) from the US border with Mexico, ready to offer food, water, and other aid to illegals who attempt to enter the country illicitly by way of the harsh desert.
- In 2012 close to 365,000 individuals were arrested by Border Patrol agents, according to the US Customs and Border Protection. The majority of these were migrant workers illegally crossing the US-Mexico border.
- Arrests of undocumented immigrants crossing the southwest border from countries other than Mexico, such as Honduras, El Salvador, and Guatemala, increased from approximately forty-five thousand in 2011 to over ninety-four thousand in 2012.

Related Organizations and Websites

American Civil Liberties Union (ACLU)
125 Broad St., 18th Floor
New York, NY 10004
phone: (212) 607-3300
website: www.aclu.org

The American Civil Liberties Union works in the courts, legislatures, and communities to preserve and defend the individual rights and liberties that the Constitution of the United States guarantees to all people. The ACLU's Immigrants' Rights Project addresses immigration issues that include workplace rights, detention and deportation, and discrimination.

American Immigration Control Foundation
PO Box 525
Monterey, VA 24465
website: www.aicfoundation.com

The American Immigration Control Foundation believes that uncontrolled immigration into the United States poses a serious threat to the nation. The organization seeks to raise public awareness through the production and distribution of numerous books, pamphlets, fact sheets, and other educational materials.

Center for Immigration Studies (CIS)
1629 K St. NW, Suite 600
Washington, DC 20006
phone: (202) 466-8185
website: www.cis.org

The Center for Immigration Studies is an independent, nonprofit research organization that publishes a variety of reports and articles that examine the social, economic, environmental, security, and economic consequences of both legal and illegal immigration. The CIS believes that debates informed by objective data will lead to better immigration policies.

Federation for American Immigration Reform (FAIR)
25 Massachusetts Ave. NW, Suite 330
Washington, DC 20001
phone: (202) 328-7004
website: www.fairus.org

The Federation for American Immigration Reform is a national nonprofit organization of citizens who share the belief that America's immigration policies must be reformed to serve the national interest. FAIR seeks to stop all illegal immigration, favors greatly enhanced border security, and supports policies that would lower legal immigration levels.

The Heritage Foundation
214 Massachusetts Ave. NE
Washington, DC 20002-4999
phone: (202) 546-4400
website: www.heritage.org

Founded in 1973, the Heritage Foundation is a research and educational institution that seeks to formulate and promote conservative public policies. It supports immigration policies that protect immigrants who enter the United States through legal channels and advocates sharp measures to deter illegal immigration.

US Citizenship and Immigration Services
Department of Homeland Security
Washington, DC 20528
phone: (202) 282-8000
website: www.uscis.gov

A branch of the US Department of Homeland Security, the US Citizenship and Immigration Services oversees lawful immigration in the United States. This includes granting all immigration and citizenship benefits and setting policies regarding who will be allowed to enter the United States. Its website provides information on current immigration laws and regulations.

For Further Research

Books

Darrell Ankarlo, *Illegals: The Unacceptable Cost of America's Failure to Control Its Borders*. Nashville: Thomas Nelson, 2010.

Jeb Bush and Clint Bolick, *Immigration Wars: Forging an American Solution*. New York: Threshold, 2013.

Julie Dowling and Jonathan Inda, eds., *Governing Immigration Through Crime: A Reader*. Stanford, CA: Stanford University Press, 2013.

Robert Lee Maril, *The Fence: National Security, Public Safety, and Illegal Immigration Along the U.S.-Mexico Border*. Lubbock: Texas Tech University Press, 2011.

Marie Friedman Marquardt et al., *Living "Illegal": The Human Face of Unauthorized Immigration*. New York: New Press, 2011.

Pilar Marrero, *Killing the American Dream: How Anti-Immigration Extremists Are Destroying the Nation*. New York: Palgrave Macmillan, 2012.

Bryan Roberts, Edward Alden, and John Whitley, *Managing Illegal Immigration to the United States: How Effective Is Enforcement?*, New York: Council on Foreign Relations, 2013.

Terry Greene Sterling, *Illegal: Life and Death in Arizona's Immigration War Zone*. Guilford, CT: Lyons, 2010.

Internet Sources

Edward Alden, "Immigration and Border Control," *Cato Journal*, Winter 2012. www.cato.org.

Federation for American Immigration Reform, "Illegal Aliens Taking U.S. Jobs (2013)," March 2013. www.fairus.org.

Immigration Policy Center, "Tackling the Toughest Questions on Immigration Reform," July 29, 2013. www.immigrationpolicy.org.

Ezra Klein, "Everything You Know About Immigration Is Wrong," *Washington Post*, August 10, 2013. www.washingtonpost.com.

Todd Miller, "War on the Border," *New York Times*, August 17, 2013. www.nytimes.com.

Robert Rector and Jessica Zuckerman, "Schumer-Corker-Hoeven Amendment Fails on Securing the Border and Halting Illegal Immigration," Heritage Foundation, June 24, 2013. www.heritage.org.

Index